The NFT Art Marketplace

THE NFT ART MARKETPLACE

Trends and Considerations

BRETT ASHLEY CRAWFORD, PH,D. & LUTIE
RODRIGUEZ

Carnegie Mellon University: ETC Press: Report

Pittsburgh, PA

CONTENTS

ACKNOWLEDGEMENTS

A big thank you to those who have helped inspire and create this short collection. Jenée Iyer, Ari Lightman, Yuxin Du, Katie Winter and Rachel Korsen. I couldn't have done it without Lutie Rodriguez to whom I am eternally grateful for her patience, attention to detail, and exquisite wordsmithing over the course of this project and throughout her time working as the Chief Editor of Research at the Arts Management and Technology Laboratory. Thank you to B Crittenden for her can-do attitude facing new technologies and her superb research over the course of myriad interviews for Let's Talk series. A special thanks to Jessica Acrie for believing in the project and always supporting the opportunity and vision. And, finally, a personal note of thanks to Sandy Murphy, without whom none of this is possible.

CHAPTER 1.

INTRODUCTION

Art, Power, Money and Disruptive Technologies

BRETT ASHLEY CRAWFORD

As Executive Director and Publisher of the Arts Management and Technology Laboratory, a research center at Carnegie Mellon University, I have a long history with technology, blockchain and the blockchain trending sweetheart—NFTs. Thus, as the world seemed to erupt with NFTs spring 2021, it seemed an appropriate time to curate a collection with commentary on the emerging, some might say exploding, world of NFTs with a focus on the arts and technology's disruptions. The following provides context to the arts marketplace, ownership, and the disruptions caused by blockchain technology, especially NFTs. This essay concludes with a short commentary on the collection and an existential thought to send you along your way down the rabbit hole of NFTs and blockchain.

TRANSACTION-BASED MARKET PLACE

The arts marketplace is an interesting thing, particularly when it comes to technology. The two are not always friendly or comfortable bedfellows. The contemporary arts world is modelled on an intermediary-based sales system. There is an artist, their work, a buyer, and someone in-between mediating the transaction. For example, a gallerist or a web platform coordinates the sale between the artist and the buyer and takes a commission for the exchange. In a brick-and-mortar marketplace, like SoHo in the 1980s, this transaction model feels normal, with a producer, gallerist, or auctioneer managing the experience and the transaction.

The digital space has injected myriad complications to this intermediated relationship. Some web platforms simply mimic the brick-and-mortar transaction pipeline. Yet other models have emerged—from low-commission platforms where artists have more control to environments that allow direct (more or less) to consumer transactions as seen in social spaces like Instagram. But, truth be told, most often the technology has benefitted the buyer or the salesperson at the transaction moment via modes of control, power, and most assuredly with respect to ownership.

WHO OWNS WHAT?

Ownership. That is a critical aspect of the arts marketplace. For economic, legal, and tax purposes, purchasing a piece of art is purchasing an asset—one that can accrue value or lose value. Thus, the question becomes who owns what, when, and where?

The artist[1] owns the work at the moment of creation. In the United States, artistic work is covered under the United States Copyright Act.[2] It was their concept and their creation. However, traditional practice holds that at the point of sale, all rights to the object are transferred to the purchaser, including future sales profits and other rights such as digital or print reproduction or merchandising. These rights can be negotiated unless the work is a work for hire. In response to visual artists' suits after changes to their work were done without their permission, the Visual

---

1. While this essay utilizes the singular artist, please note that collectives, ensembles and other artist formations are included in the singular term.

2. www.copyright.gov/title17/92chap1.html.

Artist Rights Act (VARA) of 1990 conveys moral rights. VARA "recognizes only attribution and integrity as legal causes of action. Attribution includes the rights to claim authorship of a work, to prevent attachment of an artist's name to a work which he did not create, and, where there has been a subsequent distortion, mutilation, or modification of the work prejudicial to the artist's honor or reputation, the right to disclaim authorship and to prevent identification of the artist's name with the work."[3]

Blockchain technology is one more entrant into the ecosystem of ownership. Many artists and conservators laud its ability as to provide an accurate pathway for tracking provenance, especially for newer works with known histories. All future sales are entered in the blockchain, and contract terms can also be automated. This enables artists to maintain a share in future proceeds of sales or other modes of merchandising, something often lost downstream from the moment of creation or from the first sales point.

Blockchain can further democratize the system[4] with fractured ownership, be it with NFTs or with any blockchain sales transaction. People can buy a share of a piece instead of the piece in its entirety. This tokenization of art is cognizant of the piece of art as a legal and financial asset, and much like a corporation, portions of the object, akin to shares of stock, are being bought and sold instead of the object itself.[5]

But the marketplace is designed to find means of manipulation of these systems, seemingly wanting to make more money for money's sake with the process or means provided by a mediator. For NFTs or any blockchain, that intermediate step is in the form of DAPPs.

3. www.law.harvard.edu/faculty/martin/art_law/esworthy.htm

4. agilethought.com/client-stories/democratizing-fine-art-ownership-blockchain/

5. medium.com/blockchain-art-collective/what-you-need-to-know-about-art-tokenization-and-investment-13523d3b5f1d

A DAPP stands for a decentralized app. A DAPP is similar to a web app, but using web 3.0 technology, it serves as a mediator to a blockchain(s) and runs on a smart contract. [6] Downloading a DAPP that specializes in NFT art allows you to buy, sell, or trade art on the blockchain without having to know code or blockchain technology yourself.

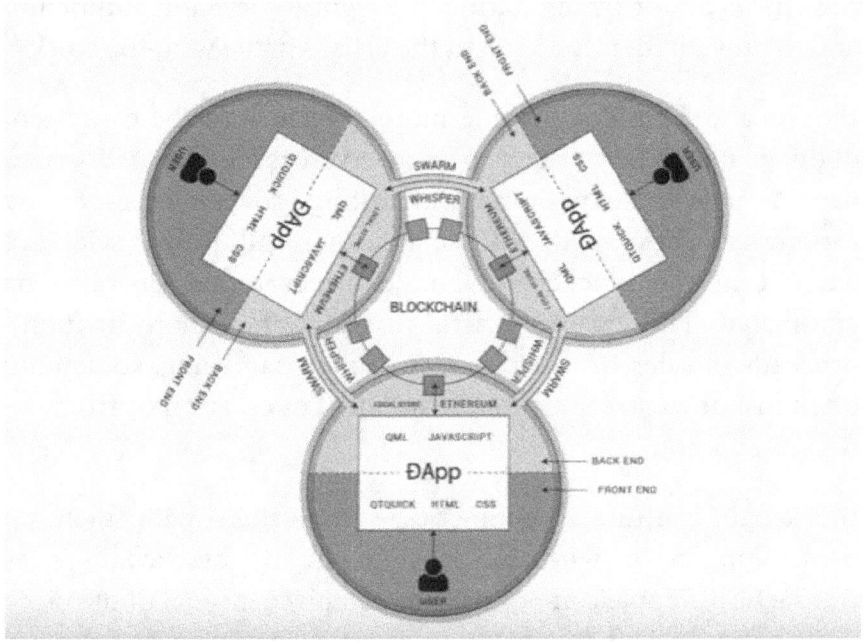

Figure 1. DAPP system visualization for a blockchain transaction.
https://blockchainhub.net/decentralized-applications-dapps/

This is the engine of NFTs. The following collection of essays offer diverse and often divergent opinions and perspectives on the future of NFTs.

The first essay orients the reader to the NFT as an expression or work of a crypto artist. Yuxin Du dissects the growth of crypto art into three phases from 2016 to present, revealing how an avant-garde experimental pastime developed into a multi-billion dollar opportunity.

6. blockchainhub.net/decentralized-applications-dapps/

The second essay focuses on the NFT art world and NFT marketplace in its 2021 current practice. Rachel Korsen explains how the NFT art marketplace is part of a bigger NFT ecosystem.

Katie Winter presents the dark side of NFTs: the climate cost of our technological collections. It is well documented that cloud computing has a significant environmental cost, but Winter investigates the cost of blockchain technology and the differences between the two dominant models—proof of work and proof of stake—that offer significantly different impacts.

Ari Lightman summarizes and concludes the collection with an opinion piece framing the past and the future of NFT's as part of both the standard digital marketplace and as part of the experience economy.

Interested readers recognize that NFT art and blockchain technology are transforming the marketplace. The impact on artists, the politics and power of dominant blockchains, and the ethics for the planet and the future of humanity raise a final question: Within the world of NFTs, who really wins? Who loses? And what's the true cost of playing the game?

CHAPTER 2.

THE ORIGIN OF CRYPTO ART

YUXIN DU

Crypto art is "a digital artwork that is published directly onto a blockchain[1] in the form of a non-fungible token (NFT),[2] which makes the ownership, transfer, and sale of an artwork possible in a secure and verifiable manner." All crypto art exists in the form of NFTs, but not all NFTs are crypto art.

1. "Blockchain," Wikimedia Foundation, last modified November 9, 2021, https://en.wikipedia.org/wiki/Blockchain.

2. "Non-fungible Token," Wikimedia Foundation, last modified November 9, 2021, https://en.wikipedia.org/wiki/Non-fungible_token.

Decentralized Ledger

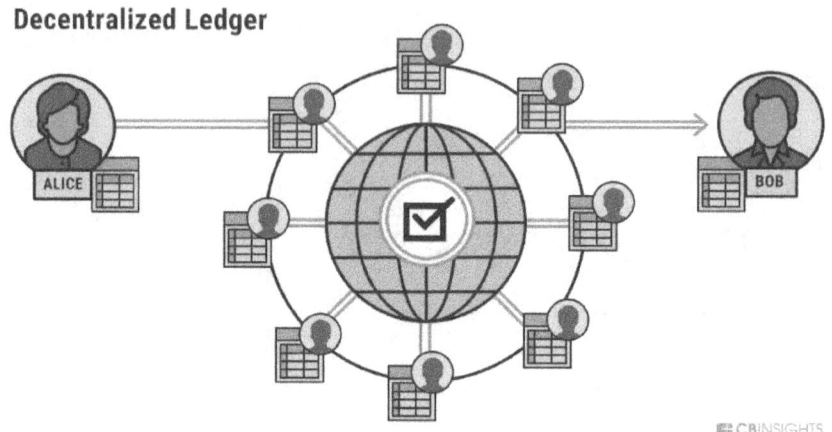

Figure 2.1 : Illustration of decentralized ledger. Source: CB Insights.

A blockchain is a digital list recording transactions. These records are called blocks and they are chained together to make a big list, which is the blockchain. Each record needs to be verified by multiple computers so that a system can't jump in and invalidate the chain or falsify a transaction. This is how cryptocurrencies like Bitcoin and Ethereum work. NFTs are tracked on blockchains to provide the owner with a proof of ownership, which is separate from copyright. The NFT is the original token that cannot be duplicated because it lives on the blockchain. Using the technology of a token acting as a digital certificate for a digital file securely held on a permanent network of computers, digital artists can sell their work like never before. Everyone can view or download the artwork, but only one individual can prove they own it.

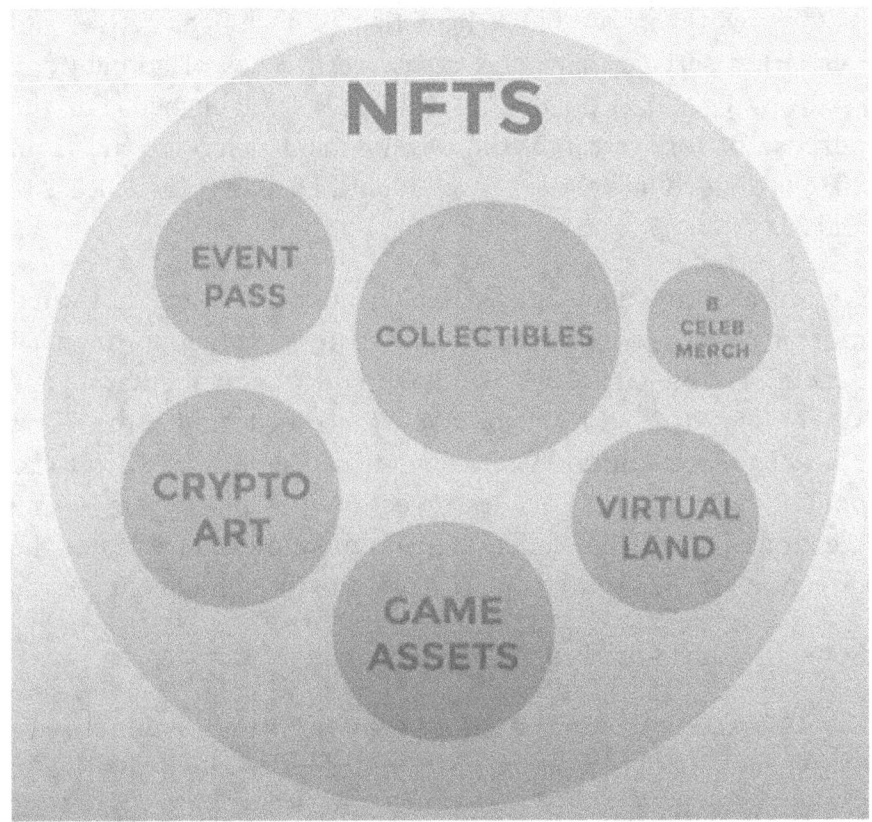

Figure 2.2: Diagram of forms of NFTs. Source: Author

HOW DID CRYPTO ART DEVELOP?

Monegraph is considered to be the first marketplace to register art on the bitcoin blockchain, and it was launched in 2014. Artists could sign into the website with their Twitter accounts and upload the URL of their digital work. In return, they received a blockchain key and value they could store in a NameCoin wallet. Monegraph detected the similarity between images and tweeted out an announcement of the ownership to commit it to public record.

In 2015 three services focusing on the arts were launched: BitchCoin, a cryptocurrency for buying art and investing in the artist; Ascribe, a project aiming to help artists claim ownership of their work on the blockchain that is no longer active; and Verisart, a service that helps create certificates of authenticity securely registered on the blockchain, were launched. For the purpose of this research, the development of crypto art from 2016 is divided into three phases, identified as crypto art 1.0, 2.0, and 3.0.

Crypto art 1.0 was a time in which members were motivated more by creative experimentation than any obvious financial benefit. Crypto art 1.0 started with Joe Looney's Rare Pepe Wallet in 2016.[3] Rare Pepe Wallet claimed to be the "first blockchain community where anyone can submit artwork to be bought, sold, traded, or destroyed on the blockchain."[4] The creation of Rare Pepe Wallet set the foundation and navigated the direction for the blockchain art market in the subsequent years.

Some firsts for Rare Pepe Wallet included:

- First blockchain community where anyone could submit artwork to be bought, sold, traded, or destroyed on the blockchain
- First to offer the above service while taking zero commission
- First to create a gift card system that allows for gifting artwork to people who do not own any cryptocurrency
- First to conceive of VIP content, such as songs and games, tied to the token in addition to the artwork
- First to move a digitally scarce artwork to a physical piece of hardware
- First to create a digital artwork tied to the blockchain that changes its representation based on what machine it

3. "Rare Pepe Wallet," Rare Pepe Wallet. Accessed November 9, 2021, https://rarepepewallet.com/.

4. Ibid.

is displayed on

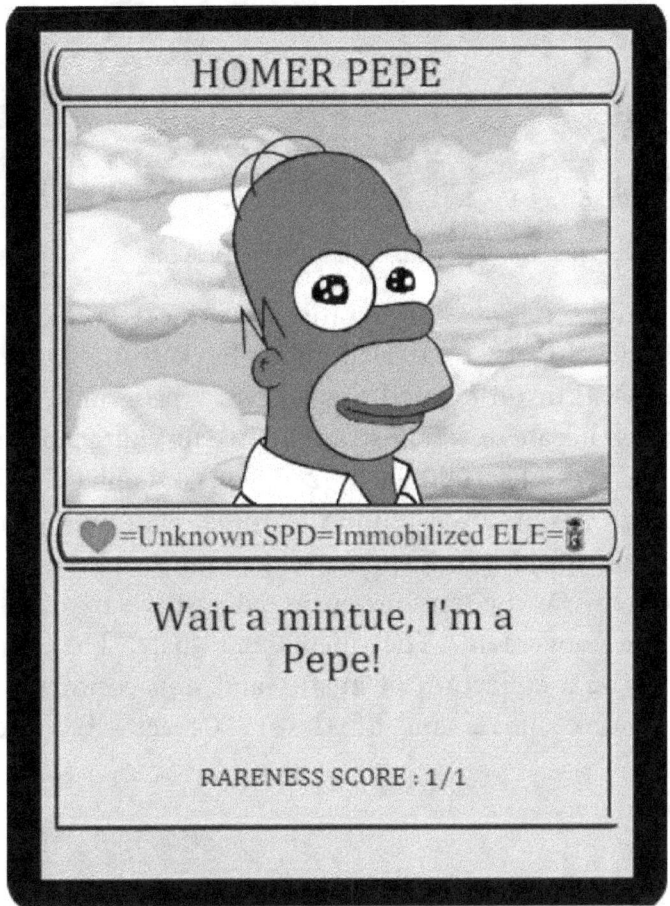

=Unknown SPD=Immobilized ELE=

Wait a mintue, I'm a Pepe!

RARENESS SCORE : 1/1

Figure 2.3: Homer Pepe (Rare Pepe, 2016).

The Rare Pepe community proved the feasibility of the blockchain art market and sold over $1.2 million worth of digital art.

With the success of Rare Pepe Wallet, many other platforms popped up, such as Crypto Punks, Dada.NYC, and Curio Cards. Because there was no template or experience for how art on the blockchain should work, all of these platforms were very different from each other.

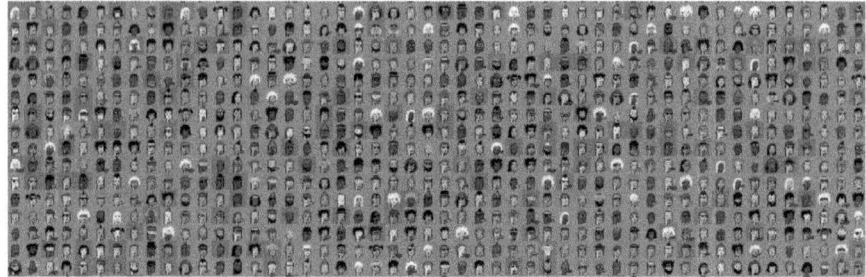

Figure 2.4: CryptoPunks Project by Larva Labs. Source: Larva Labs.

Crypto Punks is an idiosyncratic art project created by two software developers, Matt Hall and John Watkinson, in 2017.[5] Hall and Watkinson created this software program that would randomly generate different strange-looking characters. This art project consists of 10,000 24-by-24, 8-bit-style pixel art images. Each image has its own unique features. Hall and Watkinson created this project to express a raucous, anti-establishment spirit, which was a common sentiment in the early days of the blockchain movement. They explained that, "The art pieces needed to be a collection of misfits and non-conformists. The London punk movement of the 1970s felt like the right aesthetic."[6]

5. "Cryptopunks," Larva Labs, Accessed November 9, 2021
   https://www.larvalabs.com/cryptopunks.

6. Christie's. "10 things to know about CryptoPunks, the original NFTs." April 8, 2021.
   https://www.christies.com/features/10-things-to-know-about-CryptoPunks-11569-1.aspx.

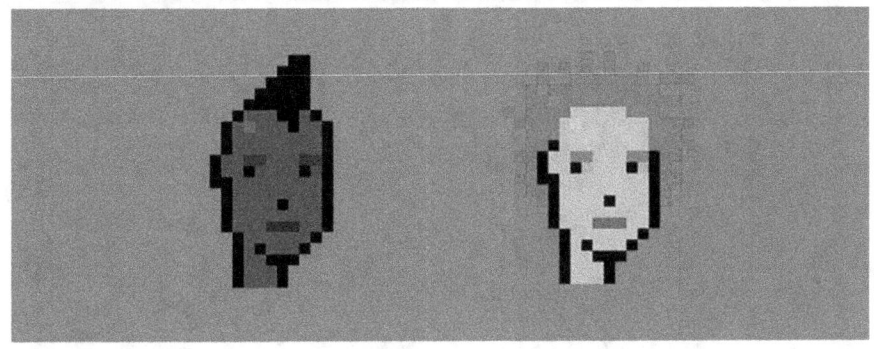

Figure 2.5: Inspired by the '70s London punk scene, many Punks have mohawks and wild hair, like CryptoPunks #532 and #602. Source: Larva Labs.

Other platforms and projects in blockchain 1.0 were also driven by the "decentralized" ethos, developed more as creative communities than by a real business model for making money.

Crypto art 2.0 started with the explosion of CryptoKitties, which is a blockchain game on Ethereum that allows players to purchase, collect, breed, and sell virtual cats. CryptoKitties players used Ethereum to buy and sell unique digital kittens. Once players had two kittens, they could breed their own digital kittens and sell them in the market. It is one of the earliest attempts to deploy blockchain technology for recreation and leisure. The game's popularity in December 2017 congested the Ethereum network. It accounted for about 25 percent of Ethereum's traffic, and more than 3.2 million transactions have occurred on CryptoKitties' smart contracts.[7]

7. Takahashi, Dean. "CryptoKitties explained: Why players have bred over a million blockchain felines." *Venture Beat*, October 6, 2018. https://venturebeat.com/2018/10/06/cryptokitties-explained-why-players-have-bred-over-a-million-blockchain-felines/.

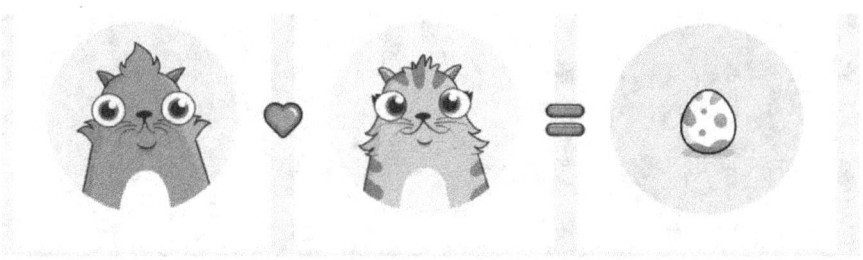

Figure 2.6: How digital kittens breed their baby. Source: CryptoKitties.

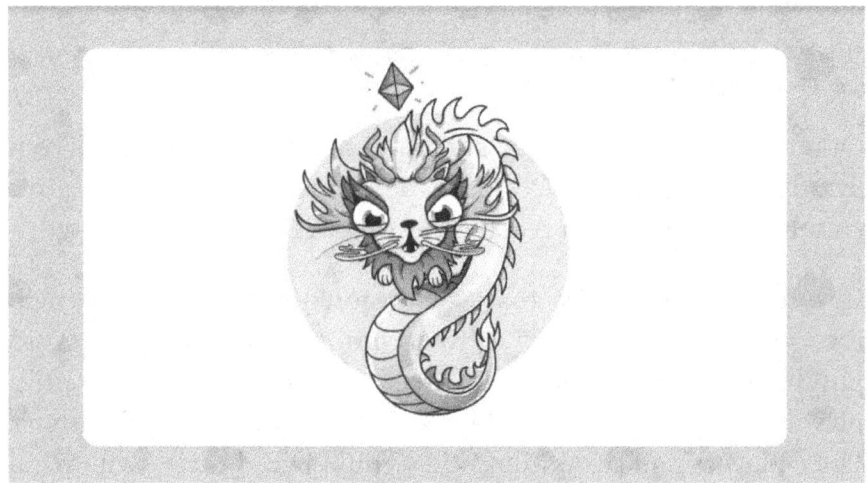

Figure 2.7: A cat named Dragon sold for 600 Ethereum (about $170,000) on the official marketplace. Source: CryptoKitties.

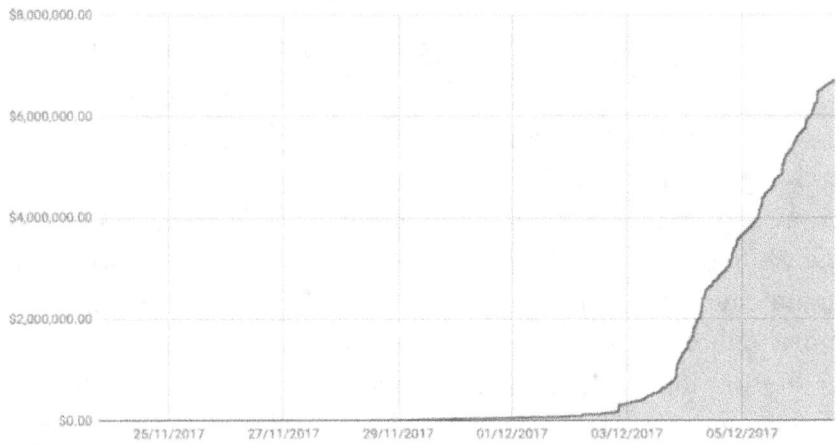
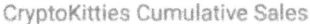

Figure 2.8: Chart showing the explosion of CryptoKitties. Source: BitDegree.

From the CryptoKitties example, people saw the opportunity to make money with digital art using blockchain and came into this marketplace based on Ethereum. The 2.0 marketplace structure was more organized and businesslike than 1.0. The 2.0 marketplaces were run more like businesses than experimental grassroots community projects. Organizations included investors, legal advisors, and advertising budgets. Some projects in 2.0 include Super Rare,[8] Known Origin,[9] Portion,[10] Rare Art Labs,[11] and Digital Objects.[12]

Crypto art 3.0 was focused on the artists' control of their work in this marketplace—for example, how their work is displayed and what artworks appear next to their pieces. Some artists cared a lot on how their work was shown and context of their work. In crypto art 3.0, artists could easily tokenize artwork without knowing code or having extra technical knowledge.

8. "SuperRare," Super Rare. Accessed March 31, 2021 https://superrare.com/activity.

9. "Known Origin," KnownOrigin. Accessed March 31, 2021 https://knownorigin.io/.

10. Digital Fashion Exhibit, Portion Museum. Accessed May 1, 2021 https://portion.io/.

11. Rare Art Labs is no longer an active website.

12. "Digital Objects," Digital Objects. Accessed May 1, 2021 https://digitalobjects.art/.

DISRUPTION IN THE ART MARKET

Crypto art disrupted the landscape of the art world in the following three ways. First, because of the blockchain's digital scarcity features, it creates a huge market for crypto collectibles and digital artwork. In the past, it was easy to duplicate and pirate digital artworks from digital artists. The piracies damage the value of artwork, have a negative effect on the economy, and might cause imbalances in the market. Things with scarcity have more value. Blockchain introduced the idea of "digital scarcity" to the digital market, which means "issuing a limited number of copies and tying them back to unique blocks proving ownership."[13]

Second, the blockchain makes fine art investment more accessible and democratic. The company Maecenas is a good example to illustrate this point. Maecenas is the first blockchain-based art investment platform. It allows "anyone to buy, sell, and trade part ownership in masterpieces on a liquid exchange, aiming to make fine art investment accessible to everyone."[14] On this platform, individuals can buy shares in paintings from well-known artists, while organizations like galleries and museums can bid their collection to raise money. The biggest advantage of using the blockchain platform is to reduce the transaction costs by cutting out the intermediary. There are some examples, shown on the Maecenas website,[15] about how it works to save money for buyers:

CONCLUSION

Knowing crypto art's origins and place in the art market, artists and arts managers can consider how it fits into their operations.

13. Jason Bailey, "The Blockchain Art market is Here," Artnome. December 27,2017. https://www.artnome.com/news/2017/12/22/the-blockchain-art-market-is-here

14. "What is Maecenas," Maecenas. https://www.maecenas.co/whats-maecenas/

15. Ibid.

Crypto art will continue to advance and evolve, so understanding its current impact will help those in the art world maximize its potential.

BIBLIOGRAPHY

Bailey, Jason. "Blockchain Art 3.0 – How To Launch Your Own Blockchain Art Marketplace." *Artnome*, February 27, 2019. https://www.artnome.com/news/2019/2/27/blockchain-art-30-how-to-launch-your-own-blockchain-art-marketplace.

Bailey, Jason. "Rare Pepe Wallet & The Birth Of Crypto Art." *Artnome*, January 25, 2018. https://www.artnome.com/news/2018/1/23/rare-pepe-wallet-the-birth-of-cryptoart.

Bailey, Jason. "The Blockchain Art Market Is Here." *Artnome*, December 27, 2017. https://www.artnome.com/news/2017/12/22/the-blockchain-art-market-is-here.

Cheng, Evelyn. "Meet CryptoKitties, the $100,000 digital beanie babies epitomizing the cryptocurrency mania." *CNBC*, December 6, 2017. https://www.cnbc.com/2017/12/06/meet-cryptokitties-the-new-digital-beanie-babies-selling-for-100k.html.

Christie's. "10 things to know about CryptoPunks, the original NFTs." April 8, 2021. https://www.christies.com/features/10-things-to-know-about-CryptoPunks-11569-1.aspx.

Constine, Josh. "Monegraph Uses Bitcoin Tech So Internet Artists Can Establish 'Original' Copies Of Their Work." *TechCrunch*, May 9, 2014. https://techcrunch.com/2014/05/09/monegraph/.

Dansky. "How to Sell CRYPTO ART – Step By Step Guide!" *YouTube* video, 4:30. March 12, 2021. https://www.youtube.com/watch?v=7dtin91E-fU.

Edward, Derek. "You're Sleeping on Crypto Art." *Medium*, September 10, 2020. https://medium.com/collab-currency/youre-sleeping-on-crypto-art-7df920ec038e.

Ehrenkranz, Melanie. "How blockchain technology reached Christie's and changed the art world along the way." *NBC*, October 27, 2020.

https://www.nbcnews.com/tech/tech-news/how-blockchain-technology-reached-christie-s-changed-art-world-along-n1244951.

Maecenas. "What is Maecenas." Accessed May 9, 2021. https://www.maecenas.co/whats-maecenas/.

Rhett / Mankind. "What is Crypto Art? A basic explanation." *YouTube* video, 3:56. Feb 11, 2021. https://www.youtube.com/watch?v=DYyW_tTPAhU.

Takahashi, Dean. "CryptoKitties explained: Why players have bred over a million blockchain felines." *Venture Beat*, October 6, 2018. https://venturebeat.com/2018/10/06/cryptokitties-explained-why-players-have-bred-over-a-million-blockchain-felines/.

The outer realm. "Crypto Art: A Brief History." March 31, 2021. https://www.theouterrealm.io/blog/crypto-art-a-brief-history.

Verisart. "Helping Creators Do Business." Accessed May 9, 2021. https://verisart.com/.

Wikipedia. "Crypto art." Last modified May 7, 2021. https://en.wikipedia.org/wiki/Crypto_art.

CHAPTER 3.

A NEW AGE OF DIGITAL ART

RACHEL KORSEN

In recent months, NFTs have had a large presence on news feeds, especially in artists' circles. NFTs, or non-fungible tokens, are "digital assets that [represent] real-world objects like art, music, in-game items and videos."[1] Because of this, they are challenging the traditional ways that people view, buy, and sell artwork. This research looks at how NFTs came to be and what artists and arts administrators should consider when utilizing this technology.

WHAT ARE NFTS?

NFTs have been around for quite some time, with the technology emerging in 2015.[2] What's really interesting about NFTs is that they aren't just a digital asset like a traditional JPG or GIF file;

1. Robyn Conti & John Schmidt, "What You Need to Know About Non-Fungible Tokens (NFTs). *Forbes*, Updated May 14, 2021. https://www.forbes.com/advisor/investing/nft-non-fungible-token/.

2. Gonzalez, Oscar. "You Can Get a Free DC X Palm NFT Tomorrow. What to Know about the Digital Tokens Now." CNET. CNET, October 4, 2021.http://www.cnet.com/personal-finance/you-can-get-a-free-dc-x-palm-nft-tomorrow-what-to-know-about-the-digital-tokensnow/#:~:text=The technology started in 2015,a big deal in February.

they are a "digital certificate of authenticity."[3] They are reminiscent of the days when people would collect baseball cards and get the players' signatures on them. With an NFT, people are able to verify the digital token's ownership. The non-fungible part of the name means that "they cannot be traded or exchanged at equivalency."[4] This is completely different from something like a bitcoin, which is a fungible cryptocurrency. Fungible cryptocurrencies are equivalent to each other, allowing them to be used for traditional commercial transactions.

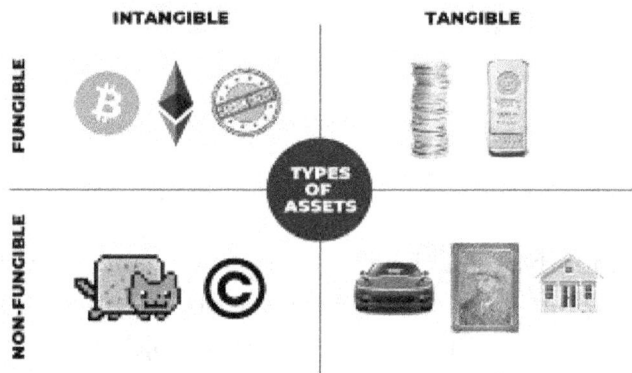

Figure 3.1 Illustration of fungible vs. non-fungible assets. Source: JingDaily.

NFTs utilize blockchain technology. Through the blockchain, NFTs can be created, bought, and traded.[5] To give some context, the blockchain is a type of database that stores information electronically. What makes the blockchain different from traditional databases is how the data is structured: "A blockchain

3. Davis, Riccardo A. "NFTs: What Are They, and How Do They Work?" Kiplinger, May 6, 2021. http://www.kiplinger.com/investing/602743/nftswhat-are-they-and-how-do-they-work#:~:text=How Do NFTs Work?,irrefutable ledger of NFT transactions.

4. Sharma, Rakesh. "Non-Fungible Token (NFT)." Investopedia, March 8, 2021. http://www.investopedia.com/non-fungible-tokens-nft-5115211.

5. Whiddington, Richard. "Decoded: NFTs, the Art World, and the Influence on Luxury." Jing Daily, March 15, 2021. https://jingdaily.com/nonfungible-tokens-nft-art-world/.

collects information together in groups, also known as blocks, that hold sets of information."[6] Each block has a set amount of storage capacity and, once the block is filled, it is "chained" to the previously filled block. A majority of NFTs exist on the Ethereum blockchain where there are "permanent digital records of all transactions using that cryptocurrency."[7]

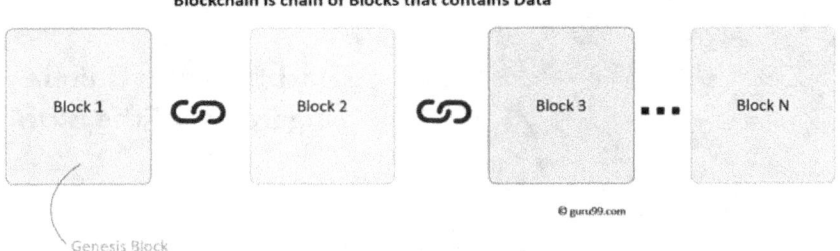

Figure 3.2. Blockchain example. Source: Guru99.

For NFTs, each block has a hash that makes each NFT unique. One way to describe a hash is comparing it to a fingerprint. The "token owner owns a record and hash code that shows ownership of the unique token associated with the particular digital asset."[8] Having a unique hash is important for maintaining security throughout the different blocks because there are concerns of hackers tampering with the blocks and changing the hashes.

6. Conway, Luke. "Blockchain Explained." Investopedia, November 4, 2021. http://www.investopedia.com/terms/b/blockchain.asp.

7. Davis, Riccardo A. "NFTs: What Are They, and How Do They Work?" Kiplinger, May 6, 2021. http://www.kiplinger.com/investing/602743/nfts-what-are-they-and-how-do-they-work#:~:text=How Do NFTs Work?,irrefutable ledger of NFT transactions.

8. "What Is a Non-Fungible Token (NFT)?" Sanction Scanner, n.d. https://sanctionscanner.com/blog/what-is-a-non-fungible-token-nft-375.

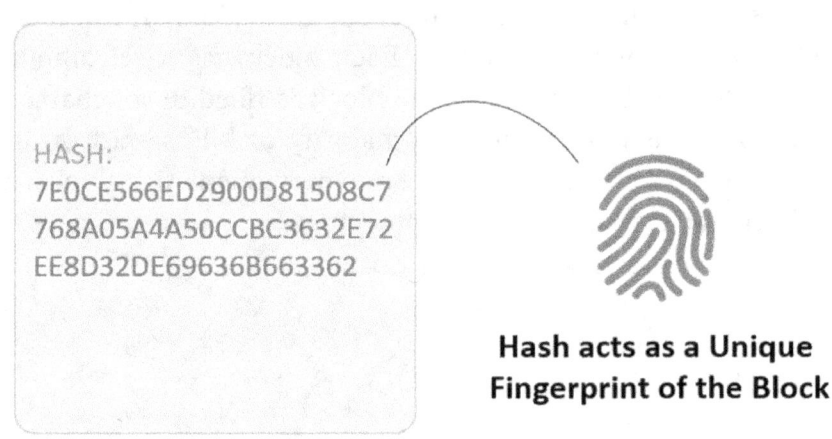

HASH:
7E0CE566ED2900D81508C7
768A05A4A50CCBC3632E72
EE8D32DE69636B663362

Hash acts as a Unique
Fingerprint of the Block

Figure 3.3. Illustration of blockchain hash. Source: Guru99.

HOW TO MAKE AN NFT

In order to get digital artwork onto the blockchain to create an NFT, it needs to be minted. Minting is "how your digital art becomes a part of Ethereum blockchain—a public ledger that is unchangeable and tamper proof."[9] In order to mint an NFT, one needs a crypto wallet. Using a site like OpenSea makes the process pretty easy.[10] When the wallet is connected, users are able to drag media files into the site in a variety of formats like JPGs, PNGs, MP4s, etcetera. The site also allows users to specify how many copies of the NFT they want generated. Once that information is set, users can click "create" and, from there, it takes a few days to be verified. After that, users are able to sell their NFTs. There are other sites, such as Rarible, on which users can create NFTs, but this is just one example of how to do so.[11] Once this whole process is completed, the minted NFT sits in the

9. "Ethereals - NFT Basics." ETHEREALS, n.d. https://ethereals.wtf/nftbasics.html.
10. "Discover, Collect, and Sell Extraordinary NFTs." OpenSea, n.d. https://opensea.io/?ref=hackernoon.com.
11. "Create and Trade Flow Blockchain NFTs on Rarible." Rarible, n.d. rarible.com/.

wallet from which users can sell their NFTs on sites like OpenSea and Rarible.

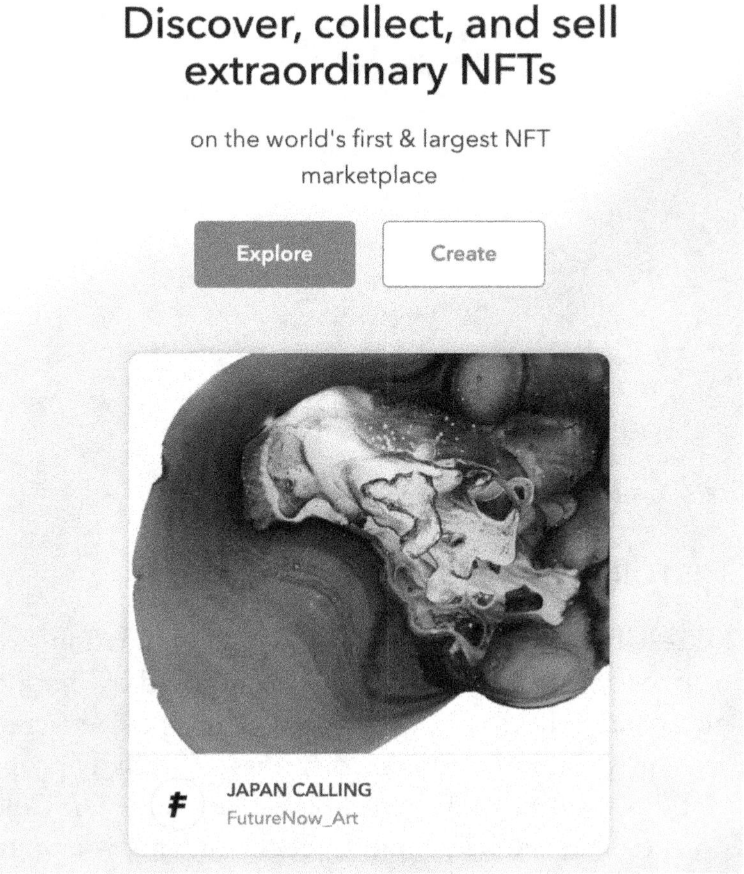

Figure 3.4. Screenshot from OpenSea's website. Source: Author.

You need an Ethereum wallet to use OpenSea.

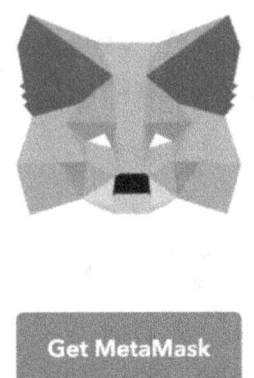

Get MetaMask

> USE A DIFFERENT WALLET

Figure 3.5. Screenshot from OpenSea's website. Source: Author.

THE HISTORY OF NFTS

In 2012-2013, Colored Coins, "a denomination of a cryptocurrency, often Bitcoin, that is repurposed by marking it with metadata," started.[12] With Colored Coins, people were able to represent several different kinds of assets, such as property, subscriptions, and digital collectibles. The value of Colored Coins was established by people agreeing on what X amount of coins would represent. In 2014, Counterparty was created as a peer-to-peer financial platform. Moving into 2015, a game called Spells of Genesis utilized the blockchain for in-game assets. In 2016, Counterparty worked with a trading card game called Force of Will to introduce their cards onto the blockchain. Additionally, a meme called Rare Pepe entered the space, and by 2017, Rare Pepes and other memes started to trade on Ethereum.

12. TechTarget Contributor. "Colored Coin." Whatis, n.d. whatis.techtarget.com/definition/coloredcoin#:~:text=A colored coin is a,represent other things of value.

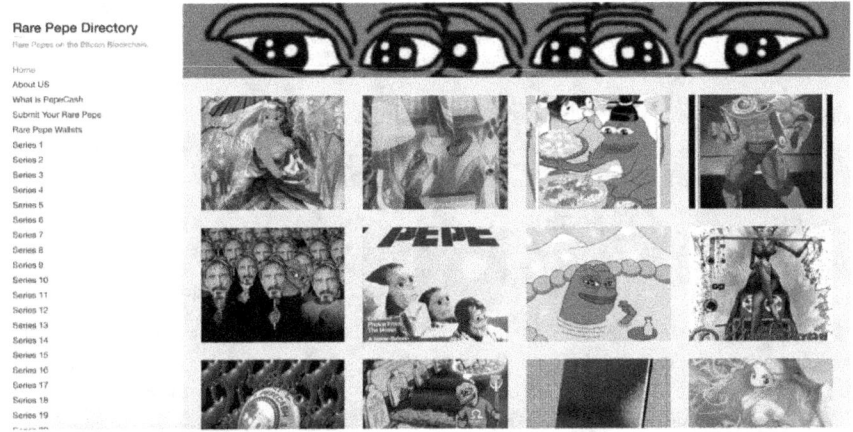

Figure 3.6. Rare Pepe memes on the Bitcoin blockchain. Source: Medium.

NFTs started to gain a lot of traction in 2017 with a game called CryptoKitties in which users could adopt and trade virtual cats on the blockchain. CryptoKitties was so popular that, due to all of the trading, it even lagged the Ethereum blockchain. Seeing the success of CryptoKitties attracted investors from a16z and Google Ventures to enter the space.[13] This represented a beginning in the NFT boom. There are now massive ecosystems for NFTs with hundreds of NFT projects as well as vibrant marketplaces like OpenSea and SuperRare.

13. Steinwold, Andrew. "The History of Non-Fungible Tokens (Nfts)." Medium. Medium, October 7, 2019.https://medium.com/@Andrew.Steinwold/the-history-of-non-fungible-tokens-nfts-f362ca57ae10.

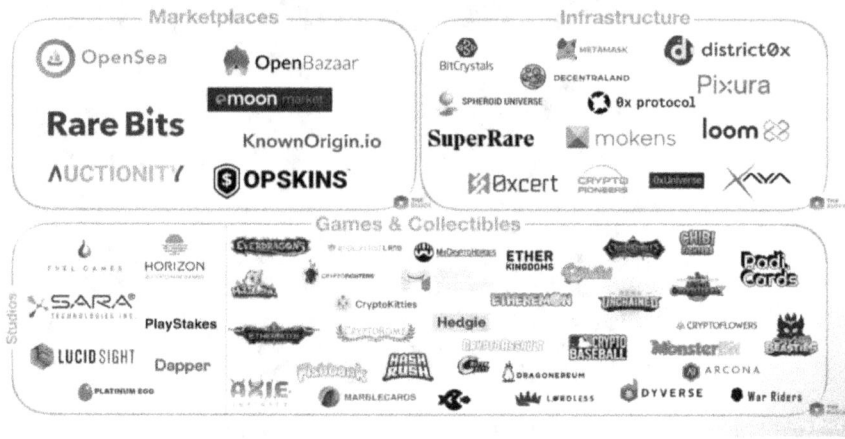

Figure 3.7. NFT ecosystems. Source: Medium.

NFTS' IMPACT ON THE ARTS INDUSTRY

With NFTs becoming even more popular, they have started to impact traditional arts spaces. The most famous example of this is when Beeple sold an NFT for $69 million. Beeple, or Mike Winkelmann, is a digital artist who had been selling and creating his artwork for more than a decade. When selling his art, he was essentially barred from traditional auction houses because digital art "can be infinitely reproduced, making the works worthless."[14] As mentioned above, NFTs allow artists to create a digital asset that is a unique one-of-one (unless, of course, the creator chooses to specify a higher amount of digital reproductions). This is what helped Beeple's art gain massive amounts of value.

Beeple's work took off in the NFT markets, which eventually attracted traditional art auction houses like Christie's. One of Beeple's pieces was minted exclusively for Christie's and the digital collage of 5,000 images was sold for $69,346,250.[15] This

14. Horowitz-Ghazi, Alexi, and Mary Childs. "The Million JPEG." NPR. NPR, March 12, 2021. http://www.npr.org/2021/03/12/976513031/the69-million-jpeg#:~:text=Mike Winkelmann, a digital artist,but there was a problem.

15. Person. "Beeple's Opus." Christies, March 11, 2021. http://www.christies.com/

was the first time in history that an auction house sold a completely digital artwork and the first time for one to accept cryptocurrency as the form of payment.

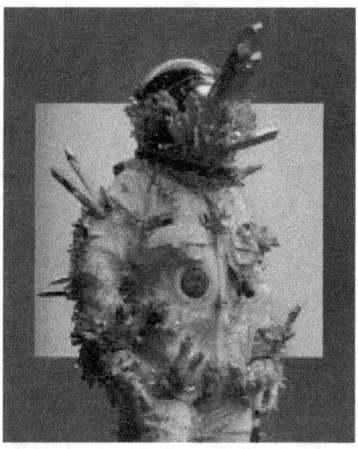

Figure 3.8. Example of Beeple's artwork. Source: CNN.

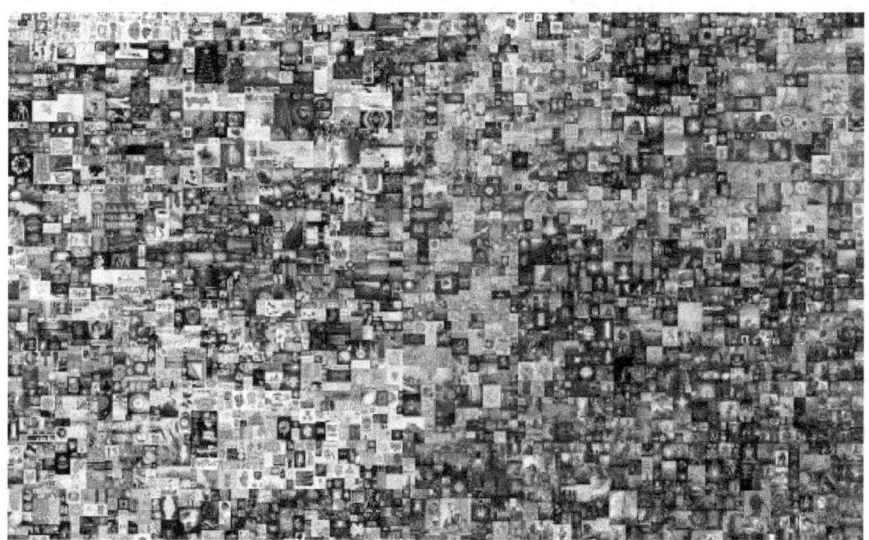

Figure 3.9. Beeple's EVERYDAYS: THE FIRST 5000 DAYS, which sold for $69,346,250. Source: Christie's.

Another example of an NFT artwork selling in an auction house

features/Monumental-collage-by-Beeple-is-first-purely-digitalartwork-NFT-to-come-to-auction-11510-7.aspx.

is the recent announcement that Sotheby's will be selling the first ever minted NFT, Kevin McCoy's *Quantum,* created in 2014.

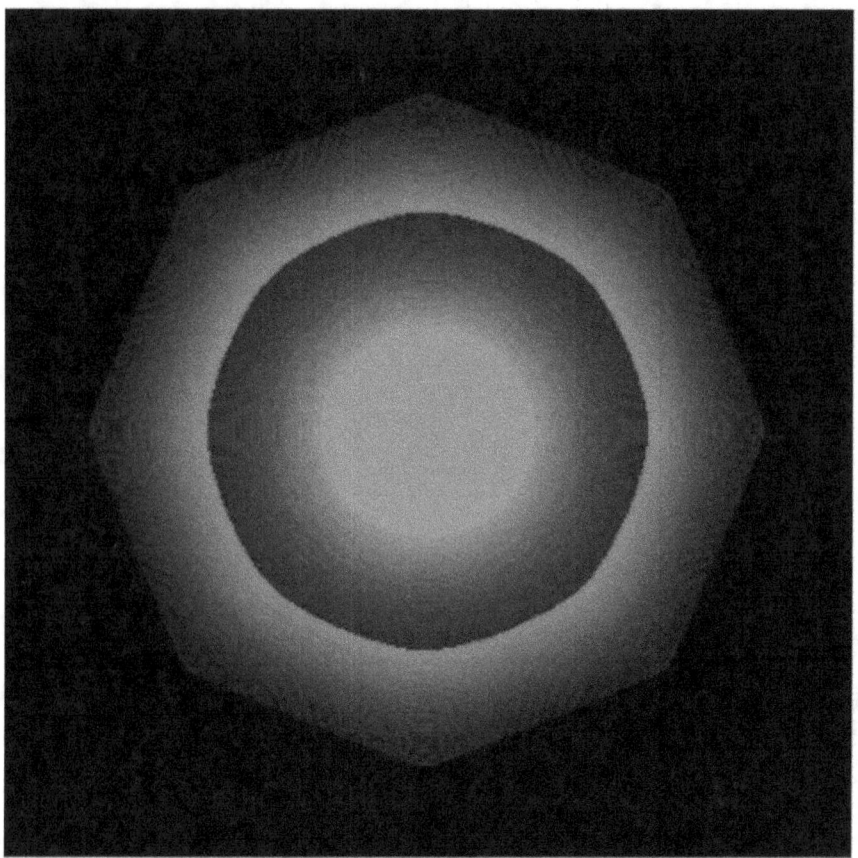

Figure 3.10. Kevin McCoy's Quantum. Source: Artnet.

Sotheby's also conducted an NFT auction of digital works by the artist Pak. Nineteen thousand seven hundred thirty-seven "cubes" were sold for $17 million during a three-day sale. This sale was a collaboration between Sotheby's and Nifty Gateway, which is an online marketplace for NFT trading. Nifty Gateway mentioned that they are "pleased that [Sotheby's] is one of the earliest adopters from the traditional and fine art world to enter the NFT space."[16] Traditionally in auctions, the buyers are

16. Kinsella, Eileen. "Sotheby's Nets Million with Its First-Ever NFT Auction (Which Included Almost 20,000 Very Fungible Works)." ArtnetNews, April 15, 2021.

anonymous, but in this auction, Sotheby's listed the handle names of the auction winners. Something simple like that shows that Sotheby's is really embracing the digital sphere even though NFT artwork is worlds apart from what it has traditionally auctioned over its lifetime.

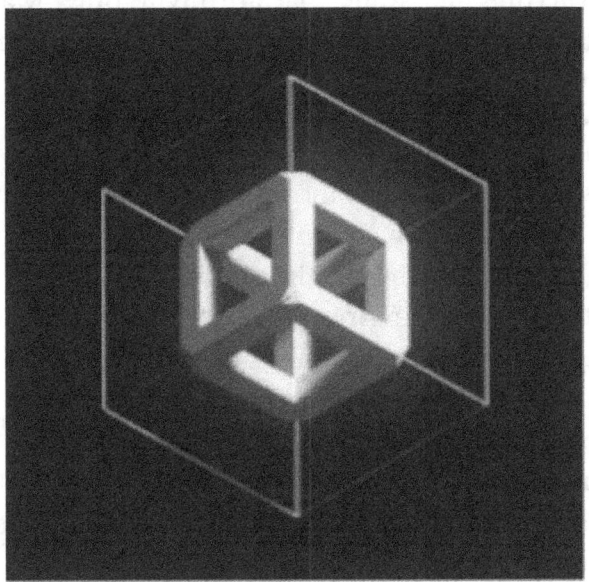

Figure 3.11 Pak's cubes. Source: Artnet.

Arts managers should take note of this shifting value of digital art as this example can be a really important shift for accessibility in the arts. With auction houses placing a larger value on digital arts, the sector may see a shift towards more digital exhibitions. In the digital space, arts managers can provide arts experiences to more people where the arts may have never been accessible to begin with. Additionally, with such a competitive landscape for artists, this provides a unique opportunity for artists to take control of their work, plan their own exhibitions digitally, and sell their uniquely minted NFT art.

NFT MARKETPLACES: PROVIDING MORE

https://news.artnet.com/market/sothebys-first-ever-sale-of-nfts-pak-and-nifty-gateway-1959276.

ACCESSIBILITY AND SECURITY FOR ARTISTS

As the NFT space continues to grow, more and more artists have become interested in getting their work onto the blockchain. There are a large variety of art marketplaces, some of which are open to everyone and some that are invite only. Marketplaces like OpenSea, Rarible, Ethernity, and FansForever all are offering marketplaces for artists to share their work.

These online marketplaces for NFTs are creating a new dynamic for artists and buyers. A lot of creators didn't necessarily understand what NFTs were but wanted to try them out as they saw NFTs gaining traction in the community. When people are buying art, they are doing research into the artists and making specific decisions about what they buy, often because "Buying in early to an artist's work comes with a sense of ownership, like having seen a now famous band at its very first gig."[17] It's a way for creators to develop their own fan base as opposed to slowly gathering a fan base through the usual social media channels like Facebook or Instagram.

Also, buyers are viewing these purchases as investments.[18] This is an important shift, especially when artists are determining the value of their work, and it's also a different viewpoint for buyers when they're deciding their next investment. If an artist becomes really popular, there may be a high resale value for the buyer. For the artist, if they already have a lot of popularity, they may have an ability to charge more. It is an interesting dynamic when you start to view the art as an investment that can be resold.

---

17. Ohlheiser, Abby. "Some Artists Found a Lifeline Selling Nfts. Others Worry It's a Trap." MIT Technology Review, March 25, 2021.http://www.technologyreview.com/2021/03/25/1021215/nft-artists-scams-profit-environment-blockchain/.

18. Yang, Peter. "A Step by Step Guide to Nfts for Creators." Creator Economy by Peter Yang, February 18, 2021.https://creatoreconomy.so/p/guide-to-nfts-for-creators.

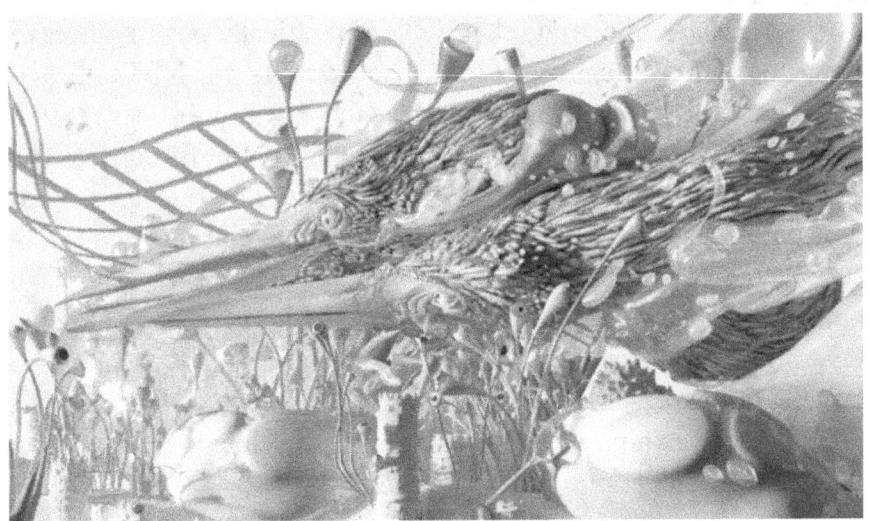

Figure 3.12 Unconditional by Sam Clover. Source: MyNorthWest.

Because of these online marketplaces, artists are now having opportunities to sell their work and many have even doubled their monthly income by selling NFTs.[19] Artists now have an ability to bypass art dealers and go directly to the market. For arts managers, there are some barriers to entering this space because there is a bit of a learning curve with the terms as well as the process of creating NFTs.

Another benefit of NFTs for artists is "tracking copyright ownership and maintaining records of creation."[20] When an artist tokenizes their work, they are able to show proof of ownership and can then transfer that token to whomever they want. There are concerns about art theft with the blockchain which will be discussed below, but the idea of the blockchain providing this level of proof could be beneficial for artists.

19. Ohlheiser, Abby. "Some Artists Found a Lifeline Selling Nfts. Others Worry It's a Trap." MIT Technology Review, March 25, 2021.http://www.technologyreview.com/2021/03/25/1021215/nft-artists-scams-profit-environment-blockchain/.
20. Bailey, Jonathan. "NFTs and Copyright." Plagiarism Today, March 16, 2021. http://www.plagiarismtoday.com/2021/03/16/nfts-andcopyright/.

There are also some NFTs that will automatically pay royalties to the artists when the piece is sold. For example, for NFTs minted on Foundation, artists receive "a 10% royalty in perpetuity, anytime a piece is resold. The royalty will be sent directly to the wallet that minted the NFT."[21] There is already an agreement structured between Foundation and other marketplaces, like Rarible and OpenSea, where all secondary market sales will receive 10% royalty if the work is resold in these markets. Overall, there are benefits with selling art as NFTs directly to buyers, but artists should still be aware of the varying costs with fees like, for example, daily fluctuating gas fees or converting other cryptocurrencies into Ethereum.[22]

There are newer platforms like Mintbase that are providing lower gas fees as compared to Ethereum. With Ethereum's growing popularity and clogged network came rising gas fees. Mintbase utilizes something called NEAR, which is a more "efficient contract execution model that requires less computation and uses a dynamic sharding approach called Nightshade."[23] Overall, there are systems being built to lessen these hidden costs and ultimately make it cheaper to make NFTs.

DISRUPTIONS CAUSED BY NFTS

While there are benefits associated with NFTs for artists, they also come with some risks. The first issue comes with the fractionalization of NFTs.[24] If there are expensive NFTs,

21. help.foundation.app/en/articles/5015275-secondary-market-royalties-on-opensea-and-rarible#:~:text=NFTs minted on Foundation receive,resold on OpenSea and Rarible.

22. Kay, Grace. "Selling Crypto Art Can Come with Huge Hidden Fees, Leading Some People to Lose Hundreds of Dollars." Business Insider, March14, 2021. http://www.businessinsider.com/nft-investing-crypto-art-what-is-a-gas-fee-explained-2021-3.

23. "Mintbase." NEAR Protocol, September 8, 2021. https://near.org/case-studies/mintbase/.

24. "NFTs Are Interesting but Fractionalized Non-Fungible Tokens (F-NFTS) May

fractionalization gives more people an opportunity to own a portion of an artwork. However, with so many people owning portions of the art comes the question of ownership. Issues can arise about who is the owner of the IP or other general contract issues. There is also a big concern that NFTs may be viewed as securities, which raises flags for financial regulators. This is mainly a concern for fractional NFTs.

Another issue with copyrights is if the person who purchased the NFT is now the copyright holder or if they only purchased a token and/or the right to resell the digital artwork they bought. The question comes down to "who owns the copyright for the work referenced in the NFT and who has the right to use the copyrighted work."[25] There are very specific nuances with copyright law, and now NFTs add an additional level to that nuance.

The third big issue is how NFTs impact the environment. The minting process for NFTs uses a process called mining which "involves complex puzzles, computing power, and a huge load of energy." Ethereum's process uses something called proof-of-work to create these digital assets.[26] Proof-of-work is an algorithm that confirms transactions, creating new blocks in the blockchain. With this process comes major negative impacts on the environment, which will be discussed further in the next section. According to the *Seattle Times*, "An average NFT has

Present Even More Challenging Legal Issues." The National LawReview, April 22, 2021. http://www.natlawreview.com/article/nfts-are-interesting-fractionalized-non-fungible-tokens-f-nfts-may-present-evenmore.

25. McDonnell, Hilary. "The Unknown Legal Future of the Art Market's New Favorite Medium: Non-Fungible Tokens ('Nfts')." HHR Art Law, April9, 2021. http://www.hhrartlaw.com/2021/04/the-unknown-legal-future-of-the-art-markets-new-favorite-medium-non-fungible-tokens-nfts/.

26. Tabuchi, Hiroko. "NFTs Are Shaking up the Art World. They May Be Warming the Planet, Too." The Seattle Times. The Seattle Times Company,April 18, 2021. http://www.seattletimes.com/business/technology/nfts-are-shaking-up-the-art-world-they-may-be-warming-the-planet-too/.

an environmental footprint of over 200 kilograms of planet-warming carbon, equivalent to driving 500 miles in a typical American gasoline-powered car."[27] This is a big concern for the future of the environment and there should be a shift in focus to solar panels or another form of green energy to power mining rigs.

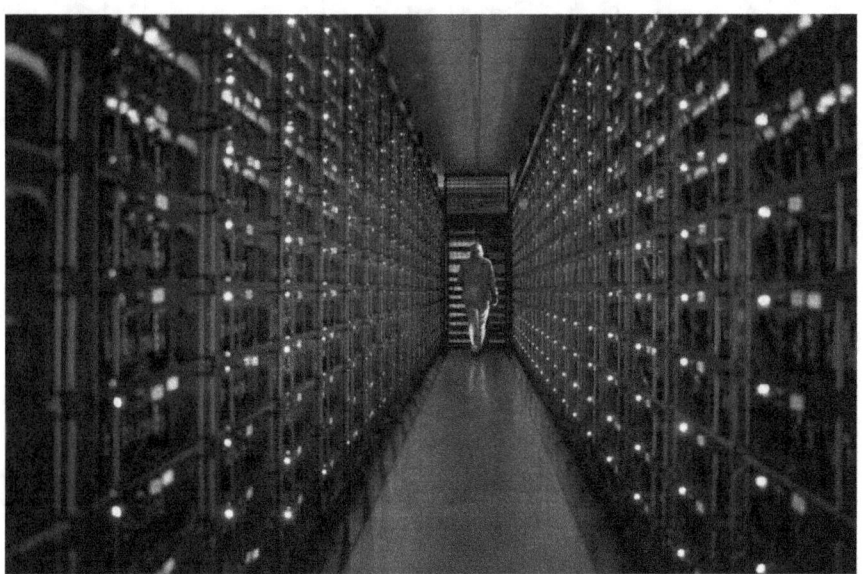

Figure 3.13 Mining rigs. Source: TIME.

CONCLUSION

Overall, NFTs are proving to be an interesting shift in the way art is bought and sold. It will be exciting to see the developments of how NFTs will expand into traditional spaces like auction houses and museums as well as what laws will come out to make sure artists maintain the rights to their minted work. Hopefully, alternative green energy sources will soon provide a power source for mining rigs. If NFTs continue to grow in popularity,

27. Tabuchi, Hiroko. "NFTs Are Shaking up the Art World. They May Be Warming the Planet, Too." The Seattle Times. The Seattle Times Company,April 18, 2021. http://www.seattletimes.com/business/technology/nfts-are-shaking-up-the-art-world-they-may-be-warming-the-planet-too/.

artists and buyers will want to be conscious of how they are impacting the environment, finding greener ways to mint and mine in crypto space.

BIBLIOGRAPHY

Adam, Georgina. "But Is It Legal? The Baffling World of NFT Copyright and Ownership Issues." *Art Newspaper*, April 6, 2021. https://www.theartnewspaper.com/analysis/but-is-it-legal-the-baffling-world-of-nft- copyright-and-ownership-questions.

Akhtar, Tanzeel. "Sotheby's Moves Into 'New World' of Digital Art and NFTs." *CoinDesk*, March 16, 2021. https://www.coindesk.com/sothebys-moves-into-new- world-of-digital-art-and-nfts.

Ayson, Samantha. "A Complete Guide to Minting an NFT." Foundation Help Center, May 8, 2021. https://help.foundation.app/en/articles/4742869-a-complete-guide-to-minting- an- nft#:~:text=Minting an NFT is how,minted" once they are created.

Baloyan, Sergey. "How To Mint Your First NFT (Non-Fungible Token) For Free." *Hacker Noon*, April 24, 2021. https://hackernoon.com/how-to-mint-your-first-nft-non-fungible-token- for-free-b42j33ek.

Bailey, Jonathan. "NFTs and Copyright." Plagiarism Today, March 16, 2021. http://www.plagiarismtoday.com/2021/03/16/nfts-and-copyright/.

Barber, Gregory. "NFTs Are Hot. So Is Their Effect on the Earth's Climate." *Wired*, March 6, 2021. https://www.wired.com/story/nfts-hot-effect-earth-climate/.

BBC. "NFT Blockchain Drives Surge in Digital Art Auctions."

BBC News, March 3, 2021. https://www.bbc.com/news/technology-56252738.

Bechara, Kristel. "NFT The Future of Digital Art: Crypto Art." NFT DIGITAL ART, April 12, 2021. https://www.atelierkristel.com/nft-digital-art/.

Boscovic, Dragan. "How Nonfungible Tokens Work and Where They Get Their Value – a Cryptocurrency Expert Explains NFTs." *The Conversation.* Accessed May 1, 2021. https://theconversation.com/how-nonfungible-tokens-work-and-where-they-get-their-value-a-cryptocurrency-expert-explains-nfts-157489.

Botz, Anneli. "Is Blockchain the Future of Art? Four Experts Weigh In." *Art Basel,* December 7, 2018. https://www.artbasel.com/news/blockchain-artworld-cryptocurrency-cryptokitties.

Built In. "Blockchain: What Is Blockchain Technology? How Does It Work?" Accessed May 8, 2021. https://builtin.com/blockchain.

Calma, Justine. "The Climate Controversy Swirling around NFTs." *The Verge,* March 15, 2021. https://www.theverge.com/2021/3/15/22328203/nft-cryptoart-ethereum-blockchain-climate-change.

Cascone, Sarah. "A Collective Made NFTs of Masterpieces Without Telling the Museums That Owned the Originals. Was It a Digital Art Heist or Fair Game?" *Artnet News,* March 22, 2021. https://news.artnet.com/art-world/global-art-museum-nfts-1953404.

Chow, Andrew R. "What Are NFTs and Why They Are Shaking Up the Art World?" *TIME,* March 22, 2021. https://time.com/5947720/nft-art/.

Clark, Mitchell. "NFTs, Explained." *The Verge*, March 11, 2021.https://www.theverge.com/22310188/nft-explainer-what-is-blockchain-crypto-art-faq.

Coggan, Georgia. "The Best NFT Artwork Created so Far." Creative Bloq. Creative Bloq, April 10, 2021. https://www.creativebloq.com/features/nft-artwork.

Conti, Robyn, and John Schmidt. "What You Need To Know About Non-Fungible Tokens (NFTs)." *Forbes Magazine*, April 29, 2021. https://www.forbes.com/advisor/investing/nft-non-fungible-token/.

Contributor, TechTarget. "What Is Colored Coin? – Definition from WhatIs.com." WhatIs.com. Accessed May 5, 2021. https://whatis.techtarget.com/definition/colored-coin#:~:text=A colored coin is a,represent other things of value.

Conway, Luke. "Blockchain Explained." *Investopedia*, November 17, 2020. https://www.investopedia.com/terms/b/blockchain.asp.

"Create and Trade Flow Blockchain NFTs on Rarible." Rarible, n.d. rarible.com/.

Dash, Anil. "NFTs Weren't Supposed to End Like This." *The Atlantic*, April 2, 2021. https://www.theatlantic.com/ideas/archive/2021/04/nfts-werent- supposed-end-like/618488/.

Davis, Riccardo A. "NFTs: What Are They, and How Do They Work?" Kiplinger, May 6, 2021. http://www.kiplinger.com/investing/602743/nfts-what-are-they-and-how-do-they-work#:~:text=How Do NFTs Work?,irrefutable ledger of NFT transactions.

Deloitte. "Blockchain Explained... in under 100 Words."

Accessed May 7, 2021. https://www2.deloitte.com/ch/en/pages/strategy-operations/articles/blockchain- explained.html.

"Discover, Collect, and Sell Extraordinary NFTs." OpenSea, n.d. https://opensea.io/?ref=hackernoon.com.

Droitcour, Brian. "How to Look at NFTs." *Art in America*, March 4, 2021. https://www.artnews.com/art-in-america/features/nft-art-1234585590/.

English, Jennifer, Toby Futter, Dave Grable, Emily Kapur, Luke Nikas, and Robert Schwartz. "NFTs: Legal Risks from 'Minting' Art and Collectibles on Blockchain." *JD Supra*. Accessed May 6, 2021. https://www.jdsupra.com/legalnews/nfts-legal-risks-from-minting-art- and-4997056/.

"Ethereals – NFT Basics." ETHEREALS, n.d. https://ethereals.wtf/nftbasics.html.

Euromoney. "What Is Blockchain?" Blockchain Explained. Accessed May 8, 2021. https://www.euromoney.com/learning/blockchain- explained/what-is-blockchain.

Fairley, Gina. "NFTs: The Pros and Cons." *ArtsHub* Australia, April 6, 2021. https://www.artshub.com.au/education/news-article/opinions-and- analysis/professional-development/gina-fairley/nfts-the-pros-and-cons- 262268#:~:text=Pros: There are two positives,separated from the NFT artwork.

Finley, Klint, and Gregory Barber. "Blockchain: The Complete Guide." *Wired*. Accessed July 9, 2019. https://www.wired.com/story/guide-blockchain/.

Foster, Max. "What Are NFTs and Can Photographers Really Benefit From Them?" Max Foster Photography. Accessed May 7, 2021. https://www.maxfosterphotography.com/gallery/what-is-an-nft-how-can- photographers-and-artists-benefit/.

Garnett, Karen, Frank Zarb, and Jeffrey Neuburger. "NFTs Are Interesting but Fractionalized Non-Fungible Tokens (F-NFTs) May Present Even More Challenging Legal Issues." *National Law Review*, April 22, 2021. https://www.natlawreview.com/article/ nfts-are- interesting-fractionalized-non-fungible-tokens-f-nfts-may-present-even-more.

Garza, Alejandro de la. "NFTs Art's Hidden Environmental Cost." *TIME*, March 18, 2021. https://time.com/5947911/nft-environmental-toll/.

Geyser, Werner. "Top NFT Marketplaces for Creators to Sell Non-Fungible Tokens." *Influencer MarketingHub*, April 26, 2021. https://influencermarketinghub.com/nft-marketplaces/.

Goldman, Jeremy. "A Primer on NFTs and Intellectual Property." *Lexology*, March 11, 2021. https://www.lexology.com/library/ detail.aspx?g=d96ed012-8789-4e87-bc1d- 70ba76569c0f.

Gonzalez, Oscar. "You Can Get a Free DC X Palm NFT Tomorrow. What to Know about the Digital Tokens Now." CNET. CNET, October 4, 2021. http://www.cnet.com/ personal-finance/you-can-get-a-free-dc-x-palm-nft-tomorrow-what-to-know-about-the-digital-tokens-now/#:~:text=The technology started in 2015,a big deal in February.

Guy, Jack. "Artwork Made of 5,000 Images Captured over 13 Years to Go on Sale in Auction House First." *CNN*, February 17, 2021. https://www.cnn.com/style/article/beeple-digital-art-auction-scli-intl/index.html.

Horowitz-Ghazi, Alexi, and Mary Childs. "The $69 Million JPEG." NPR. NPR, March 12, 2021. http://www.npr.org/2021/ 03/12/976513031/the-69-million-jpeg#:~:text=Mike Winkelmann, a digital artist,but there was a problem.

IBM. "What Is Blockchain Technology – IBM Blockchain."

Accessed May 7, 2021. https://www.ibm.com/topics/what-is-blockchain.

Jiang, Yaling. "How China's Art Market Embraced NFTs." *Artsy*, May 4, 2021. https://www.artsy.net/article/artsy-editorial-chinas-art-market-embraced-nfts.

Kastrenakes, Jacob. "Beeple Sold an NFT for $69 Million." *The Verge*, March 11, 2021. https://www.theverge.com/2021/3/11/22325054/beeple-christies-nft-sale-cost- everydays-69-million.

Kay, Grace. "Selling Crypto Art Can Come with Huge Hidden Fees, Leading Some People to Lose Hundreds of Dollars." Business Insider, March 14, 2021. http://www.businessinsider.com/nft-investing-crypto-art-what-is-a-gas-fee-explained-2021-3.

Kinsella, Eileen. "Sotheby's Nets $17 Million with Its First-Ever NFT Auction (Which Included Almost 20,000 Very Fungible Works)." Artnet News, April 15, 2021. https://news.artnet.com/market/sothebys-first-ever-sale-of-nfts-pak-and-nifty-gateway-1959276.

McDonnell, Hilary. "The Unknown Legal Future of the Art Market's New Favorite Medium: Non- Fungible Tokens ('NFTs')." *HHR Art Law*, April 9, 2021. https://www.hhrartlaw.com/2021/04/the-unknown-legal-future-of-the-art-markets- new-favorite-medium-non-fungible-tokens-nfts/.

"Mintbase." NEAR Protocol, September 8, 2021. https://near.org/case-studies/mintbase/.

Morris, David Z. "Where Does Your Blockchain Art Really Live?" *Fortune*, March 10, 2021. https://fortune.com/2021/03/10/are-your-nfts-on-the-wrong-blockchain/.

Newsdesk, Dazn. "What Are NFTs? How Do I Buy Them? How Can I Sell Them?: DAZN News US." *DAZN News*, May 8, 2021. https://www.dazn.com/en-US/news/boxing/what-are-nfts-how-do-i-buy-them-how-can-i-sell-them/6lzungqnrak01lbd4pu4c6oc9

"NFTs Are Interesting but Fractionalized Non-Fungible Tokens (F-NFTS) May Present Even More Challenging Legal Issues." The National Law Review, April 22, 2021. http://www.natlawreview.com/article/nfts-are-interesting-fractionalized-non-fungible-tokens-f-nfts-may-present-even-more.

Ohlheiser, Abby. "Is the New Boom in Digital Art Sales a Genuine Opportunity or a Trap?" *MIT Technology Review*, March 25, 2021. https://www.technologyreview.com/2021/03/25/1021215/nft-artists-scams-profit- environment-blockchain/.

Patterson, Dan. "Blockchain Company Buys and Burns Banksy Artwork to Turn It into a Digital Original." *CBS News*, March 4, 2021. https://www.cbsnews.com/news/banksy-nft-injective-destroy-art-digital-token/.

Person. "Beeple's Opus." Christies, March 11, 2021. http://www.christies.com/features/Monumental-collage-by-Beeple-is-first-purely-digital-artwork-NFT-to-come-to-auction-11510-7.aspx.

Pires, Samantha. "Crypto Art: How Artists Are Selling Their Work on Blockchain." *My Modern Met*, February 10, 2021. https://mymodernmet.com/crypto-art-blockchain/.

PwC. "Making Sense of Bitcoin, Cryptocurrency and Blockchain." Accessed May 7, 2021. https://www.pwc.com/us/en/industries/financial-services/fintech/bitcoin-blockchain-cryptocurrency.html.

Rapoza, Kenneth. "NFTs Are Increasingly Taking Us Into A World Of Make Believe." *Forbes Magazine*, May 2, 2021. https://www.forbes.com/sites/kenrapoza/2021/05/02/nfts-are-increasingly-taking-us-   into-a-world-of-make-believe/?sh=2f9089326ccf.

Richardson, Jim. "Museum NFT 'Art Heist' Sees Famous Artworks Sold Online." *MuseumNext*, March 13, 2021. https://www.museumnext.com/article/nft-art-heist-museums/.

Sanction Scanner. "What Is a Non-Fungible Token (NFT)?" Accessed May 7, 2021. https://sanctionscanner.com/blog/what-is-a-non-fungible-token-nft- 375#:~:text=What makes an NFT unique,asset interoperability acr oss multiple platforms.

Sharma, Rakesh. "Non-Fungible Token (NFT)." *Investopedia*, March 18, 2021. https://www.investopedia.com/non-fungible-tokens-nft-5115211.

Shimon, Yonatan Ben. "How Non-Fungible Tokens are Revolutionizing the Art World." Nasdaq, May 3, 2021. https://www.nasdaq.com/articles/how-non-fungible-tokens-are- revolutionizing-the-art-world-2021-05-03.

Small, Zachary. "As Auctioneers and Artists Rush Into NFTs, Many Collectors Stay Away." *New York Times*, April 28, 2021. https://www.nytimes.com/2021/04/28/arts/design/nfts-art-collectors-copyright.html.

Steinwold, Andrew. "The History of Non-Fungible Tokens (Nfts)." Medium. Medium, October 7, 2019. https://medium.com/@Andrew.Steinwold/the-history-of-non-fungible-tokens-nfts-f362ca57ae10.

Tabuchi, Hiroko. "NFTs Are Shaking up the Art World. They May Be Warming the Planet, Too." *Seattle Times*, April 18, 2021. https://www.seattletimes.com/business/technology/nfts-are-shaking-up-the-art-world-they-may-be-warming-the-planet-too/.

TechTarget Contributor. "Colored Coin." Whatis, n.d. whatis.techtarget.com/definition/colored-coin#:~:text=A colored coin is a,represent other things of value.

Thaddeus-johns, Josie. "What Are NFTs, Anyway? One Just Sold for $69 Million." *New York Times*, March 11, 2021. https://www.nytimes.com/2021/03/11/arts/design/what-is-an-nft.html.

"What Is a Non-Fungible Token (NFT)?" Sanction Scanner, n.d. https://sanctionscanner.com/blog/what-is-a-non-fungible-token-nft-375.

Whiddington, Richard. "The Potential And Pitfalls Of NFTs In The Museum Sphere." *Jing Culture and Commerce*, April 30, 2021. https://jingculturecommerce.com/cuseum-nfts-in-museum-sector-webinar-takeaways/.

Willis, Simon. "Crypto Millionaires' Love of NFTs Is a Boon for the Aging Art Market-but Galleries May Miss Out." *Fortune*, April 14, 2021. https://fortune.com/2021/04/14/nft- non-fungible-token-art-crypto-art-market-galleries-auction-houses/ .

Yang, Peter. "A Step by Step Guide to Nfts for Creators." Creator Economy by Peter Yang, February 18, 2021. https://creatoreconomy.so/p/guide-to-nfts-for-creators.

CHAPTER 4.

FUELING THE GLOBAL FLAME

A Look at the Long-Term Sustainability of NFTs

KATIE WINTER

WHAT ARE NFTS?

Nonfungible tokens, abbreviated NFTs, became a widely known sensation when the artwork *EVERYDAYS: THE FIRST 5000 DAYS* (shown below) by artist Mike Winklemann, known as Beeple,[1] sold at Christie's for $69.3 million USD on March 11, 2021.[2]

---

1. Beeple, "ABOUT," accessed May 10, 2021, http://www.beeple-crap.com/about.

2. Christie's, "Beeple (b. 1981) EVERYDAYS: THE FIRST 5000 DAYS," 2021, https://onlineonly.christies.com/s/beeple-first-5000-days/beeple-b-1981-1/112924.

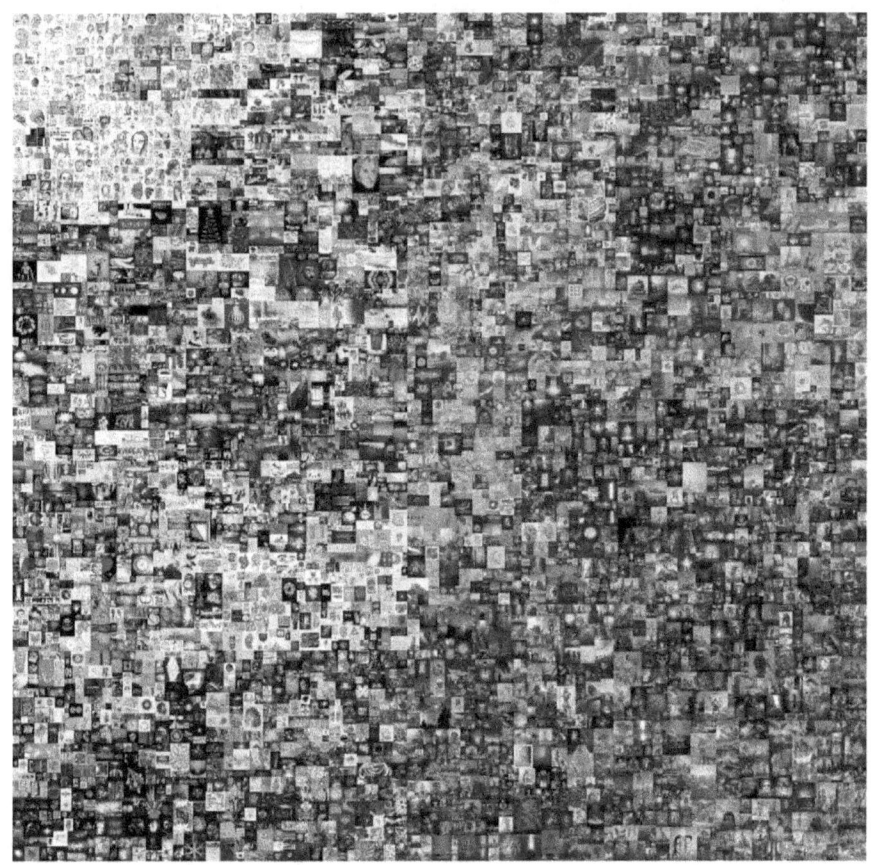

Figure 4.1: EVERYDAYS: THE FIRST 5000 DAYS by Beeple. Source: MakersPlace.

NFTs are unique, identifiable digital assets, differentiated from other digital files by authenticity.[3] For example, NFTs are essentially a digital certificate of authenticity that represent one's ownership of the asset on that blockchain. Because these tokens are stored on the blockchain, they are publicly verifiable and traceable, granting an element of prestige to the buyer.[4] While anyone can still view and download images of Beeple's artwork, only the buyer possesses the NFT, holding the value and

3. Riccardo A Davis, "NFTs: What Are They, and How Do They Work?," Nasdaq, May 6, 2021, http://www.nasdaq.com/articles/nfts:-what-are-they-and-how-do-they-work-2021-05-06.

4. Rahul Nambiampurath, "NFTs Explained: What Are NFTS and How Do They Work?," *Be In Crypto*, April 8, 2021, https://beincrypto.com/learn/nfts-explainer/.

authentic ownership of the asset. Thus, NFTs being non-fungible means that they cannot be readily exchanged for another NFT, granting the additional element of scarcity.[5] As an example, while two $1 bills could be easily swapped, the same cannot be said about two NFTs. NFTs' non-fungible characteristic is visually depicted in the diagram below.

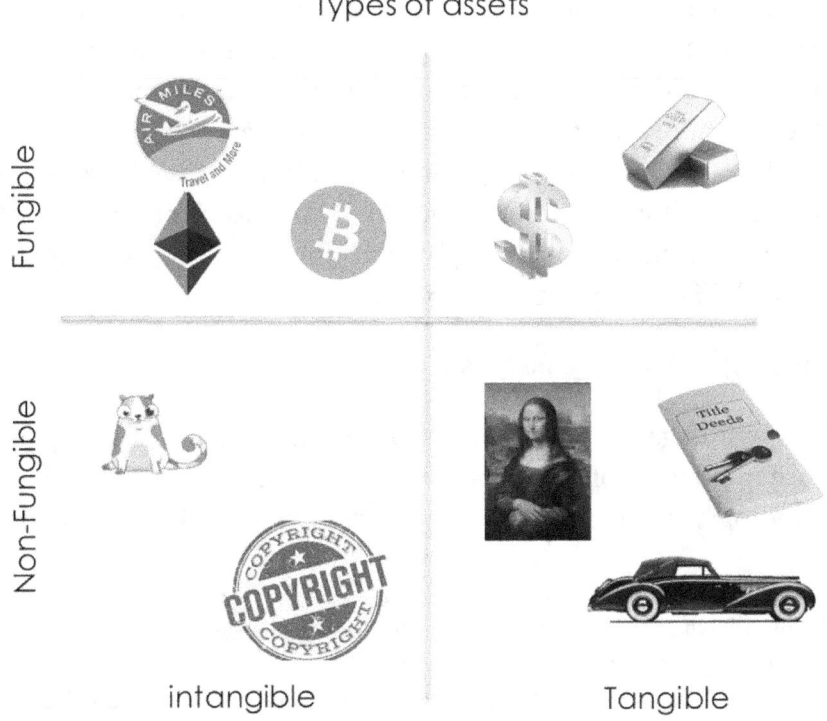

Figure 4.2: Diagram of fungibility and tangibility. Source: BlockChainArtExchange.

HOW DO NFTS WORK?

NFTs serve as a public ledger, a fixed record of data "blocks," representing a variety of transactions, such as a purchase of bitcoin or transfer of NFT art.[6] Blocks are added to a chain

---

5. Mike Jenkins, "Non Fungible Tokens: Beginners Guide to NFTs," Coin Bureau, August 13, 2020, http://www.coinbureau.com/education/non-fungible-tokens-nft/.

6. Tiffany C Li, "Bitcoin, NFTs and Other Crypto Fads Are Destroying Our Planet,"

through crypto mining, a process of computers solving cryptographic equations through high-powered computers.[7] The *New York Times* further breaks down the mining process and explains blocks in a video (see footnote).[8]

According to NASDAQ, most NFTs reside on the Ethereum cryptocurrency blockchain.[9] The NFT world utilizes Ethereum because the Ethereum blockchain allows for the building of smart contracts, also called decentralized applications.[10] Ethereum operates on a proof-of-work system, the same as Bitcoin, where coin mining relies on computers solving complex "puzzles," and the only way to increase solving theses "puzzles" is through more computational power.[11] For those interested, you can watch a video explaining blockchain technology on the the *New York Times'* YouTube channel.[12]

HOW DID NFTS COME TO BE?

NFTs, while gaining vast attraction in the past year, come from a larger history of digital collectibles, trades, and blockchain technology. DigitalTrends[13] attributes NFTs to technologies

MSNBC, March 16, 2021, http://www.msnbc.com/opinion/bitcoin-nfts-other-crypto-fads-are-destroying-our-planet-n1261139.

7. Casey Crane, "What Is Crypto Mining? How Cryptocurrency Mining Works," InfoSec Insights, December 4, 2020, https://sectigostore.com/blog/what-is-crypto-mining-how-cryptocurrency-mining-works/.

8. https://youtu.be/0B3sccDYwuI

9. Riccardo A Davis, "NFTs: What Are They, and How Do They Work?"

10. Rahul Nambiampurath, "NFTs Explained: What Are NFTS and How Do They Work?,".

11. Jessica Lloyd, "Proof of Work and Proof of Stake Explained," *Be In Crypto*, June 1, 2020, https://beincrypto.com/learn/proof-of-work-explained/.

12. *How Cryptocurrency Works, YouTube*, 2018, https://www.youtube.com/watch?v=0B3sccDYwuI&t=1s.

13. Luke Dormehl, "A Very Brief History of Non Fungible Tokens or Nfts," Digital Trends, March 10, 2021, http://www.digitaltrends.com/features/what-are-nfts-non-fungible-tokens-history-explained/.

from 2012 and 2014 like Colored Coins[14] and Counterparty,[15] both concepts to use blockchain technology for trading assets and digital collectibles. Similarly, CryptoPunks[16] and CryptoKitties[17] became more popular tradable and collectible blockchain projects with a gaming element. It is important to note, various other gaming platforms, such as an Ethereum-based VR platform, Decentraland,[18] inspired the framework[19] for selling, buying, and collecting digital assets. NFTs have since boomed in 2021 with various digital assets being sold as NFTS, including a *New York Times* article,[20] various films,[21] tweets,[22] and even live performances.[23] This boom can be seen in the diagram below featuring relative search volumes from 0 to 100, with 100 being the maximum value during a defined time period.

14. Steve Walters, "What Are Colored Coins? The Ultimate Guide," *Unblock*, April 27, 2018, https://unblock.net/what-are-colored-coins/.

15. Counterparty, "Counterparty Extends Bitcoin in New and Powerful Ways," October 13, 2017, https://counterparty.io/.

16. Larva Labs, "CryptoPunks," accessed May 10, 2021, http://www.larvalabs.com/cryptopunks.

17. CryptoKitties, "Collect and Breed Digital Cats!," accessed May 10, 2021, http://www.cryptokitties.co/.

18. Decentraland, "Welcome to Decentraland," accessed May 10, 2021, https://decentraland.org/.

19. Luke Dormehl, "A Very Brief History of Non Fungible Tokens or Nfts."

20. Kevin Roose, "Buy This Column on the Blockchain!," *The New York Times*, March 24, 2021, http://www.nytimes.com/2021/03/24/technology/nft-column-blockchain.html.

21. Chris Lindahl, "It's Not a Movie, It's an NFT! How Hollywood Is Flirting with the Non-Fungible Token," IndieWire, April 8, 2021, http://www.indiewire.com/2021/04/nft-hollywood-non-fungible-token-1234628823/.

22. Weston Blasi, "Twitter CEO Jack Dorsey Is Selling His First Tweet - Bidding Has Reached .5 Million," MarketWatch, March 8, 2021, http://www.marketwatch.com/story/twitter-ceo-jack-dorsey-is-selling-his-first-tweet-bidding-is-at-2-5-million-11615226262.

23. Vasja Veber, "What Does a Live Gig NFT Mean for the Music Industry?," *Digital Music News*, April 22, 2021, http://www.digitalmusicnews.com/2021/04/21/viberate-live-gig-nfts/.

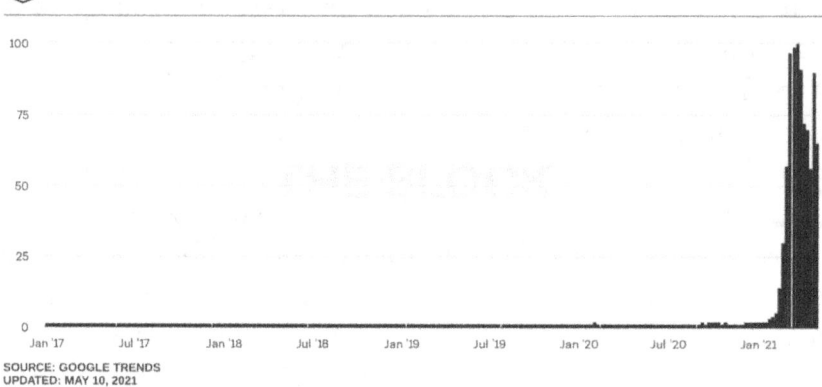

Google Search Volume - NFT

SOURCE: GOOGLE TRENDS
UPDATED: MAY 10, 2021

Figure 4.3: A graph featuring the Google Search volume for the term NFT. Source: The Block.

How do NFTs affect the environment?

Because Ethereum utilizes the proof-of-work method, computers must rapidly work to solve cryptographic puzzles, generating numbers in a race of trial and error.[24] According to the *New York Times'* reporting on blockchain mining, miners in mid-April of 2021 made over 170 quintillion attempts per second to produce new blocks.[25] Only the miner who arrives at the correct answer will get their asset added to the blockchain and receive currency back. While this system is designed to be transparent and competitive, the process uses significantly large amounts of energy.[26] While blockchain energy consumption varies between platforms, Ethereum currently consumes more electricity and produces a larger carbon footprint than some countries. The diagram 4.4 breaks this down.

24. Hiroko Tabuchi, "NFTs Are Shaking up the Art World. They May Be Warming the Planet, Too.," The *New York Times*, April 13, 2021, http://www.nytimes.com/2021/04/13/climate/nft-climate-change.html.

25. Hiroko Tabuchi, "NFTs Are Shaking up the Art World. They May Be Warming the Planet, Too."

26. Hiroko Tabuchi, "NFTs Are Shaking up the Art World. They May Be Warming the Planet, Too."

Whether or not NFTs increase emissions themselves is still very much debated. *The Verge* argues that, without NFTS, miners would still mine Ethereum and pollute.[27] NFT marketplace SuperRare further argues that Ethereum mining is similar to a train: even if everyone stops buying NFTs—"buying their seats" on the train—the train will still be running and using the same energy. However, Joseph Pallant, founder of the nonprofit Blockchain for Climate Foundation,[28] compares trying to calculate the environmental effects of buying and selling NFTs to trying to calculate one's share of emissions from a commercial plane flight, meaning that one single person is not responsible for the overall emissions, yet the overall demand for the industry does cause more emissions.[29]

27. Justine Calma, "The Climate Controversy Swirling around Nfts," The Verge, March 15, 2021, http://www.theverge.com/2021/3/15/22328203/nft-cryptoart-ethereum-blockchain-climate-change.

28. Blockchain for Climate Foundation, "Vision," 2021, http://www.blockchainforclimate.org/our-vision.

29. Justine Calma, "The Climate Controversy Swirling around Nfts."

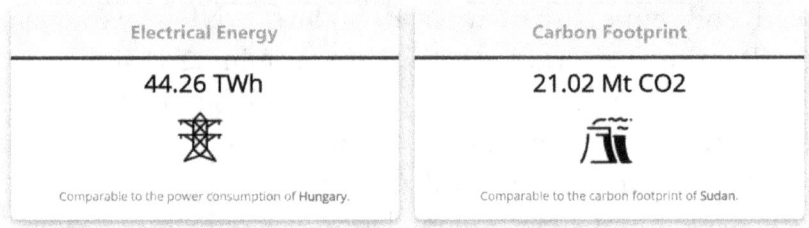

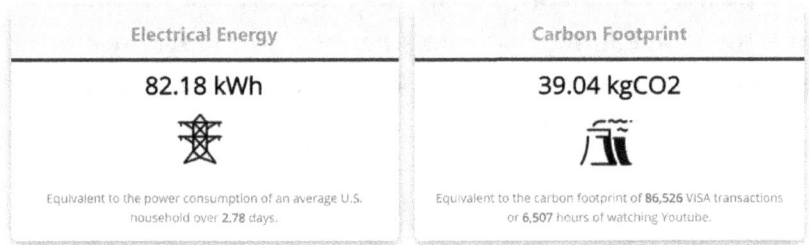

Figure 4.4: An illustration showing both the annualized total and single transaction electrical energy consumption and carbon footprint of the Ethereum network. Source: Digiconomist.

WILL NFTS' ENVIRONMENTAL IMPACT CHANGE?

Recently, more artists, such as Joanie Lemercier, are calling for a larger movement towards sustainable NFTs.[30] *TIME* argues that while crypto mining energy could come from renewable resources, fossil fuel conversion produces larger profits.[31] Many users in the crypto art community argue that the technology needs to switch to the proof-of-stake blockchain process from the current proof-of-work blockchain process.[32] While proof-of-

30. . Joanie Lemercier, "The Carbon Drop," Studio Joanie Lemercier, March 22, 2021, joanielemercier.com/the-carbon-drop/#:~:text=by Joanie Lemercier; in activism CryptoArt; posted mars,friends and artists to try addressing this issue.

31. Alejandro De La Garza, "NFTS Art's Hidden Environmental Cost," *Time*, March 18, 2021, https://time.com/5947911/nft-environmental-toll/.

32. Melanie Ehrenkranz, "The Crypto Art Community Is Having a Sustainability

work now relies on heavy computation energy from computers solving puzzles, proof-of-stake would not use these mathematical puzzles but, according to Be In Crypto, instead rely on a "deterministic probability influenced by the number of coins staked at a specific moment."[33] These proof-of-work and proof-of-stake concepts are discussed more in depth in the following video by Blockgeeks.

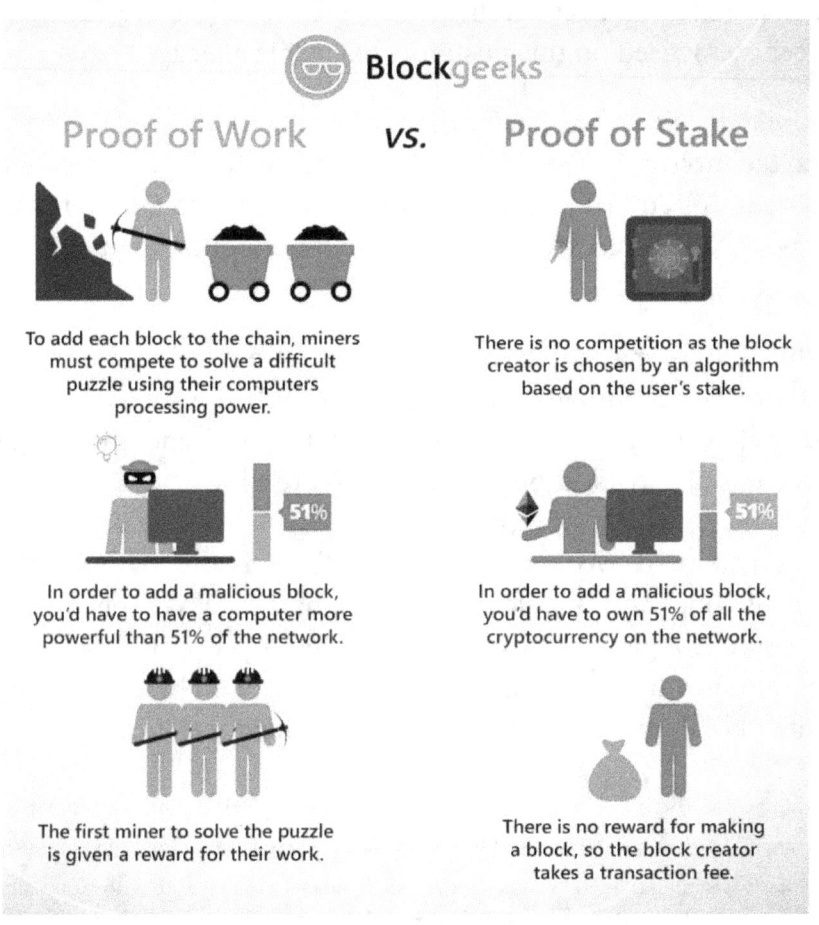

Figure 4.5: Difference between Proof of Stake and Proof of Work. Source: Blockgeeks

Reckoning," NBC News, March 24, 2021, http://www.nbcnews.com/tech/tech-news/crypto-art-community-sustainability-reckoning-rcna481.

33. Jessica Lloyd, "Proof of Work and Proof of Stake Explained."

ARE NFTS HERE TO STAY IN THE ARTS FIELD?

While NFTs took the arts market by storm in the beginning of 2021, with the environmental impact of blockchain technology coming to light, more artists and groups have not only been criticized but have also begun calling out the technology and not participating.[34] Others are calling on more long-term changes, such as renewable resourcing for crypto-mining. NowThis Earth recently focused on this push for renewable energy.

Similar to NowThis Earth, more individuals such as columnist and technology lawyer Tiffany Li are calling for legislative action to asses this environmental impact. In fact, Li further emphasizes in her MSNBC article, "The crypto fad might not burn out—but our planet could."[35]

While long-term concerns mainly entail environment impact, artists are becoming more concerned with the safety of NFTs as well. Various platforms like Bolster Blog[36] and the Verge[37] have urged artists to be cautious of increasing scams regarding NFT theft and artist impersonation. Artists like Derek Laufman have had their work minted as NFTs and sold without their permission.[38] Artist Liadoodles emphasizes, "We need more protection regarding copyright issues and property. We've had these issues for years and the NFT is just the cherry on top."[39] Thus, NFTs, while currently booming, have yet to reach their

34. Tiffany C Li, "Bitcoin, NFTs and Other Crypto Fads Are Destroying Our Planet."

35. Tiffany C Li, "Bitcoin, NFTs and Other Crypto Fads Are Destroying Our Planet."

36. Abhilash Garimella, "NFT Scams Part 1: 5 NFT Scams You Need to Know," Bolster Blog, April 3, 2021, https://bolster.ai/blog/5-nft-scams-you-need-to-know/.

37. Bijan Stephen, "NFT Mania Is Here, and so Are the Scammers," *The Verge*, March 20, 2021, https://www.theverge.com/2021/3/20/22334527/nft-scams-artists-opensea-rarible-marble-cards-fraud-art.

38. Bijan Stephen, "NFT Mania Is Here, and so Are the Scammers."

39. Cass Marshall, "NFTs Are Generating Huge Paydays for Some Artists, Others Feel under Siege," Polygon, March 12, 2021, https://www.polygon.com/22327806/nft-artists-online-theft-non-fungible-token.

final form. This technology, while still relatively new, has many downfalls to still overcome to prove its place as a long-term technology in the art world.

Arts organizations, since joining the NFT trend, have faced backlash from artists. In fact, ArtStation recently announced their jump into buying and selling NFTs. In response, thousands of artists took to Twitter, slamming the decision and threatening to delete their accounts.[40] Museums have similarly been called out by the public and activists for their acceptance of oil company sponsorships.[41] NFTs present a similar controversy to arts organizations, especially ones not only concerned about their role in climate change but with their overall reputation in the public eye. Some smaller NFT platforms, such as Hic Et Nunc, have moved to blockchains such as Tezos, claiming to become the "first-ever environment-friendly marketplace for digital raribles."[42] Other platforms have promised carbon offsets,[43] yet critics still argue these moves are not enough.[44] Regardless, both large arts organizations, like ArtStation, and smaller platforms, like Hic Et Nunc, must be aware of this public concern and growing reputation of NFTs.

40. News Bureau, "Artstation Rethinks NFT Crypto Art Push after Environmental Backlash," OTCPM24, March 10, 2021, https://www.otcpm24.com/2021/03/10/artstation-rethinks-nft-crypto-art-push-after-environmental-backlash/.

41. Kathleen Massara, "Environmental Activists Focus on Museums That Take Oil Money," The New York Times, October 9, 2018, http://www.nytimes.com/2018/10/09/business/environmental-activists-take-on-oil-money.html.

42. Vladislav Sopov, "Tezos-Based NFT Platform Hic Et Nunc Celebrates Leonardo Da Vinci's Birthday, Here's How," U Today, April 4, 2021, u.today/tezos-based-nft-platform-hic-et-nunc-celebrates-leonardo-da-vincis-birthday-heres-how#:~:text=Hic Et Nunc, which is Latin for Here,in the world by the *New York Times*.

43. SuperRare Team, "No, CryptoArtists Aren't Harming the Planet," *SuperRare*, March 3, 2021, https://medium.com/superrare/no-cryptoartists-arent-harming-the-planet-43182f72fc61.

44. Hiroko Tabuchi, "NFTs Are Shaking up the Art World. They May Be Warming the Planet, Too."

EFFECTS ON INDIVIDUAL ARTISTS

While NFTs have been controversial, it is important to note the benefit to individual artists. Smaller artists with NFTs have not only been able to increase their exposure and recognition but also receive money for digital artworks that before did not have such a large market. In fact, artist Vakseen argues that NFTs specifically help Black artists get the financial recognition they deserve.[45] New NFT art clubs, such as Black NFT Art, have made over $700,000 working together selling NFTs.[46] Addressing the controversial element of NFTs, digital designer and artist Gareth Stangroom stated to the New York Times, "Why is it when the little guys get a foothold, everyone's on their case about the ethics of it—instead of criticizing the big players that have been abusing our planet for decades?"[47]

Ultimately, both individual artists and arts organizations must engage with NFTs within their own ethical comfort level. Looking at the long-term viability of NFTs, software startup 2MuchCoffee emphasizes, "we've had non-fungible tokens used for everything from selling skins for online games to tracing food in supply chains...What is different this time is how much mainstream it got—and each evolution adds a layer of accessibility. In this light, NFTs are revolutionary."[48] While NFTs have burst into the mainstream in 2021, more evolutionary changes will need to occur for this technology to stay mainstream in the long run.

45. Hero Collective, "Why NFTs Are Benefiting Artists of Color the Most," accessed May 11, 2021, https://herocollective.co/why-nfts-are-benefiting-artists-of-color-the-most/.

46. Hero Collective, "Why NFTs Are Benefiting Artists of Color the Most."

47. Hiroko Tabuchi, "NFTs Are Shaking up the Art World. They May Be Warming the Planet, Too."

48. 2muchcoffee, "NFTs: FAD or Future? Uncovering the Truth of The Hype," 2MuchCoffee, May 6, 2021, https://2muchcoffee.com/blog/nfts-fad-or-future-uncovering-the-truth-of-the-hype/

BIBLIOGRAPHY

2muchcoffee, "NFTs: FAD or Future? Uncovering the Truth of The Hype," 2MuchCoffee, May 6, 2021, https://2muchcoffee.com/blog/nfts-fad-or-future-uncovering-the-truth-of-the-hype/.

Beeple. "ABOUT." Accessed May 10, 2021. https://www.beeple-crap.com/about.

Blockchain for Climate Foundation. "Vision." 2021. https://www.blockchainforclimate.org/our-vision.

Christie's. "Beeple (b. 1981) EVERYDAYS: THE FIRST 5000 DAYS." 2021. https://onlineonly.christies.com/s/beeple-first-5000-days/beeple-b-1981-1/112924.

Blasi, Weston. "Twitter CEO Jack Dorsey Is Selling His First Tweet – Bidding Has Reached $2.5 Million." *MarketWatch*, March 8, 2021. https://www.marketwatch.com/story/twitter-ceo-jack-dorsey-is-selling-his-first-tweet-bidding-is-at-2-5-million-11615226262.

Blockchain Art Exchange. "To Fungible or Not to Fungible." November 21, 2019. https://blockchainartexchange.com/is-art-fungible-what-is-non-fungible/.

Calma, Justine. "The Climate Controversy Swirling around Nfts." The Verge, March 15, 2021. http://www.theverge.com/2021/3/15/22328203/nft-cryptoart-ethereum-blockchain-climate-change.

Clark, Mitchell. "NFTs, Explained." *The Verge*, March 3, 2021. https://www.theverge.com/22310188/nft-explainer-what-is-blockchain-crypto-art-faq.

Counterparty. "Counterparty Extends Bitcoin in New and Powerful Ways." October 13, 2017. https://counterparty.io/.

Crane, Casey. "What Is Crypto Mining? How Cryptocurrency Mining Works." *InfoSec Insights*, December 4, 2020. https://sectigostore.com/blog/what-is-crypto-mining-how-cryptocurrency-mining-works/#:~:text=The term crypto mining means gaining cryptocurre ncies by,a public record (ledger) known as a blockchain.

CryptoKitties. "Collect and Breed Digital Cats!" Accessed May 10, 2021. https://www.cryptokitties.co/.

Davis, Riccardo A. "NFTs: What Are They, And How Do They Work?" Nasdaq, May 6, 2021. https://www.nasdaq.com/articles/nfts:-what-are-they-and-how-do-they-work-2021-05- 06.

Decentraland. "Welcome to Decentraland." Accessed May 10, 2021. https://decentraland.org/.

De La Garza, Alejandro. "NFTs Art's Hidden Environmental Cost." *TIME*, March 18, 2021. https://time.com/5947911/nft-environmental-toll/.

Dormehl, Luke. "A Very Brief History of Non Fungible Tokens or NFTs." *Digital Trends*, March 10, 2021. https://www.digitaltrends.com/features/what-are-nfts-non-fungible- tokens-history-explained/.

E Hacking News. "Centre of Attraction for Scammers: NFTs." April 3, 2021. https://www.ehackingnews.com/2021/04/centre-of- attraction-for-scammers-nfts.html.

Ehrenkranz, Melanie. "The Crypto Art Community Is Having a Sustainability Reckoning." NBC News, March 24, 2021. http://www.nbcnews.com/tech/tech-news/crypto-art-community-sustainability-reckoning-rcna481.

Fairs, Marcus. "The Environmental Impact of NFTs Is 'Horrible' Says Architect Chris Precht." *Dezeen*, April 1, 2021. https://www.dezeen.com/2021/03/29/environmental-impact-nfts- horrible-architect-chris-precht/.

Garimella, Abhilash. "NFT Scams Part 1: 5 NFT Scams You Need to Know." *Bolster Blog*, April 3, 2021. https://bolster.ai/blog/5-nft-scams-you-need-to-know/.

Hero Collective. "Why NFTs Are Benefiting Artists of Color the Most." Accessed May 11, 2021. https://herocollective.co/why-nfts-are-benefiting-artists-of-color-the-most/.

How Cryptocurrency Works. YouTube, 2018. https://www.youtube.com/watch?v=0B3sccDYwuI&t=1s.

Jenkins, Mike. "Non Fungible Tokens: Beginners Guide to NFTs." Coin Bureau, August 13, 2020. https://www.coinbureau.com/education/non-fungible-tokens-nft/.

Larva Labs. "CryptoPunks." Accessed May 10, 2021. https://www.larvalabs.com/cryptopunks.

Lemercier, Joanie. "The Carbon Drop." Studio Joanie Lemercier, March 22, 2021. joanielemercier.com/the-carbon-drop/#:~:text=by Joanie Lemercier; in activism CryptoArt; posted mars,friends and artists to try addressing this issue.

Li, Tiffany C. "Bitcoin, NFTs and Other Crypto Fads Are Destroying Our Planet." *MSNBC*, March 16, 2021. https://www.msnbc.com/opinion/bitcoin- nfts-other-crypto-fads-are-destroying-our-planet-n1261139.

Lindahl, Chris. "It's Not a Movie, It's an NFT! How Hollywood Is Flirting with the Non-Fungible Token." *IndieWire*, April 8, 2021. https://www.indiewire.com/2021/04/nft- hollywood-non-fungible-token-1234628823/.

Lloyd, Jessica. "Proof of Work and Proof of Stake Explained." *Be In Crypto*, June 1, 2020. https://beincrypto.com/learn/proof-of-work-explained/. \

MakersPlace. "Beeple: EVERYDAYS: THE FIRST 5000 DAYS." 2021. https://makersplace.com/beeple/5000-days/.

Marshall, Cass. "NFTs Are Generating Huge Paydays for Some Artists, Others Feel under Siege." Polygon, March 12, 2021. https://www.polygon.com/22327806/nft-artists-online-theft-non-fungible-token.

Massara, Kathleen. "Environmental Activists Focus on Museums That Take Oil Money." *New York Times*, October 9, 2018. https://www.nytimes.com/2018/10/09/business/environmental-activists-take-on-oil- money.html.

McIntosh, Rachel. "Creating an NFT from Start to Finish: Here's What You Need to Know: Finance Magnates." Finance Magnates, March 18, 2021. https://www.financemagnates.com/cryptocurrency/news/creating-an-nft- from-start-to-finish-heres-what-you-need-to-know/#:~:text=However, many artists and analysts agree that% 20despite,identified as the future of the creative economy.

Nambiampurath, Rahul. "NFTs Explained: What Are NFTs and How Do They Work?" *Be In Crypto*, April 8, 2021. https://beincrypto.com/learn/nfts-explainer/.

News Bureau. "Artstation Rethinks NFT Crypto Art Push after Environmental Backlash." OTCPM24, March 10, 2021. https://www.otcpm24.com/2021/03/10/artstation-rethinks-nft-crypto-art-push-after-environmental-backlash/.

NewsNFT. "Are NFTs a Good Long Term Investment? On Ownership & Long-Term Viability." April 9, 2021.

https://www.newsnft.com/are-nfts-a-good-long-term-investment-on-ownership-long-term-viability/.

Roose, Kevin. "Buy This Column on the Blockchain!" *New York Times*, March 24, 2021. https://www.nytimes.com/2021/03/24/technology/nft-column-blockchain.html.

Rosic, Ameer. "Proof of Work vs Proof of Stake: Basic Mining Guide." *Blockgeeks*, June 19, 2020. https://blockgeeks.com/guides/proof-of-work-vs-proof-of-stake/.

Sopov, Vladislav. "Tezos-Based NFT Platform Hic Et Nunc Celebrates Leonardo Da Vinci's Birthday, Here's How." U Today, April 4, 2021. u.today/tezos-based-nft-platform-hic-et-nunc-celebrates-leonardo-da-vincis-birthday-heres-how#:~:text=Hic Et Nunc, which is Latin for Here,in the world by The New York Times.

Stephen, Bijan. "NFT Mania Is Here, and so Are the Scammers." The Verge, March 20, 2021. https://www.theverge.com/2021/3/20/22334527/nft-scams-artists-opensea-rarible-marble-cards-fraud-art.

SuperRare Team. "No, CryptoArtists Aren't Harming the Planet." *SuperRare*, March 3, 2021. https://medium.com/superrare/no-cryptoartists-arent-harming-the-planet-43182f72fc61.

Tabuchi, Hiroko. "NFTs Are Shaking up the Art World. They May Be Warming the Planet, Too." *Seattle Times*, April 16, 2021. https://www.seattletimes.com/business/technology/nfts-are-shaking-up-the-art-world-they-   may-be-warming-the-planet-too/.

Tabuchi, Hiroko. "NFTs Are Shaking Up the Art World. They May Be Warming the Planet, Too." *New York Times*, April 13, 2021. https://www.nytimes.com/2021/04/13/climate/nft-climate-change.html.

The Block. "Web Traffic Metrics for Popular Crypto Currency Exchanges." 2021. https://www.theblockcrypto.com/data/alternative-crypto-metrics/web-traffic.

Veber, Vasja. "What Does a Live Gig NFT Mean for the Music Industry?" *Digital Music News,* April 22, 2021. https://www.digitalmusicnews.com/2021/04/21/viberate-live-gig-nfts/.

Walters, Steve. "What Are Colored Coins? The Ultimate Guide." *Unblock,* April 27, 2018. https://unblock.net/what-are-colored-coins/.

CHAPTER 5.

NFT—EVOLUTION OR REVOLUTION?

ARI LIGHTMAN

NFTs will continue to evolve and permeate society. They are not revolutionary in terms of how consumer interact with brands and creators around digital art and collectables. If we strip away the technical components powering NFTs namely the blockchain, hashing technology, public and private keys and proof of work assessment, NFTs simply represent an evolution of trends that have been in place for quite some time.

The most evident is the direct connection between creators and purchasers, between artists and their audience, between sports teams or players and their fans. This direct connection is valuable, efficient and transferrable. By stripping out the intermediaries, whether an agent or an auction house, more revenue flows back to creators rather than dolling out a percentage of the transaction to a variety of intermediaries that enable the transaction. In enabling a direct connection between artist and fan, the speed associated with transfer becomes almost instantaneous. In addition, the holder of the work, collectable, consumable that has been tokenized can then transfer that seamlessly to another party without having to go through the traditional mechanisms. This includes the provenance associated with the item, a history of transactions and any experiential component that is associated with owning the NFT.

Another trend involves hyper personalization and the experiential economy. Audiences and fans are willing to pay premium pricing for items that confer differentiation and added benefit associated with the holder of an item. When the Kings of Leon [1] did a NFT drop and provided right to purchase first row tickets to any upcoming concert associated with the purchase of the NFT, they encapsulated the desire of certain fans of the band to purchase a right to an experience along with a digital good. In fact, the right could possibly be more valuable to the title holder than the digital good itself. This ability to wrap an experience (could be access to the creator, acknowledgment from the industry, specialized content not available to the general public) provides uniqueness to the title holder of the NFT

The last trend is transferability and more autonomy to the title holder. As a title holder to an NFT, I can sell or transfer the NFT to another party without surcharges or brining in a variety of experts to guarantee its authenticity. Authenticity, provenance and any added experiential component is already associated with the NFT. The non-fungible nature implies that there is a decision between the buyer and seller as to the worth of the NFT without appraisers or other specialists needed to determine worth or value. If we apply this concept from digital art to sports collectables, I can sell or transfer a digital trading card or a tokenized ticket to a game to another relatively effortless and all the rights associated with owning the NFT get transferred as well. It also opens a larger potential audience for the NFT than in a traditional manner. This will continue to expand as more

1. Emma Nolan, "What are NFTs? Kings of Leon Sell New Album as Non-Fungible Tokens," *Newsweek*, March 5, 2021.

options and assurances become available to increase access and bring in consumers who might currently remain skeptical[2]

The last item to mention is data. A digital transaction as opposed to a physical transfer of an art piece or collectable provides a plethora of data to both parties. In a traditional physical transaction, a good portion of the process steps and information around the transaction need to be digitized. There is also the question of which party has access to the data and in most cases each part including intermediaries hold different pieces of data that make up the story associated with the transaction. With an NFT transaction, that data becomes open and available without a great deal of stipulations. In some case this data becomes more valuable that the revenue associated with the transaction. It provides information as to the audience and prospective consumers, what they are looking for in terms of experiential components, a complete transactional ledger associated with ownership and use as well as many other pieces of information that traditionally were not available or traditionally difficult to piece together to provide a complete picture on the history of the transaction, ownership, externalities, etc. In addition, added metadata can be embedded into the NFT to provide additional information associated with source, time, collaborators, etc. that will stay with the NFT from one owner to another.[3]

There are several issues associated with NFTs including the environmental costs associated with proof of stake ownership, the heavy reliance on the Ethereum for purchasing NFTs – Ethereum as well as other cryptocurrencies have fluctuated widely in value and issues associated with privacy and security. I have no doubt that these issues will be worked out and addressed to further push NFTs into different industries and opened to the mainstream. We have witnessed this in other digital

2. Ethan Spears, "A Clear Explanation of NFTs and Their Potential Impact on Sports", *LA Times*, July 15, 2021.
3. Kyle Tut, "Who Is Responsible for NFT Data?," Medium, April. 2020

technologies including digital payment mechanisms. The trends supporting NFT adoption are powerful, economically valuable and in demand by large portions of the population. NFTs will continue to evolve and address the issues associated with crypto currencies, blockchain based transactions, privacy and security. We will see deepening of NFT based transactions with digital goods and physical and/or digital experiences as well as tokenized physical goods. These will expand from collectables to consumables, from artists to producers specialized unique NFT drops to common everyday mechanisms associated with purchasing a digital or tokenized physical good. The value for producers and creators along with the increasing demand from consumers is too strong to ignore.

BIBLIOGRAPHY

Nolan, Emma. "What are NFTs? Kings of Leon Sell New Album as Non-Fungible Tokens." *Newsweek*, March 5, 2021.

Spears, Ethan. "A Clear Explanation of NFTs and Their Potential Impact on Sports." *LA Times*, July 15, 2021.

Tut, Kyle. "Who Is Responsible for NFT Data?," Medium, April, 2020.

ABOUT THE ARTS MANAGEMENT AND TECHNOLOGY LABORATORY

The Arts Management and Technology Laboratory (AMT Lab) answers the "how" and "why" of implementation for particular technology solutions. These ideas are presented via case studies of best practices, product reviews, interviews, and national surveys. Our researchers do the deep dive for you providing a unique and in-depth understanding of where technology is going in the arts management sector.

MISSION

A research center of Carnegie Mellon University's Master of Arts Management program, AMT Lab serves as an exchange, a catalyst for innovative ideas, and a conduit for knowledge circulating at the intersection of arts, management, and technology.

IMPACT

AMT Lab provides current and future arts managers, technologists, and researchers with existing best practices and emerging technologies that allow for a direct impact on their work and their organization. Through online and off-line engagement, AMT Lab is a resource that leads to the innovative, effective and efficient integration of technology in the cultural and creative enterprise space.

VALUES

Knowledge | Dialogue | Innovation | Rigor | Creativity | Open-Mindedness | Curiosity | Relevancy | Practicality

ABOUT THE ETC PRESS

The ETC Press was founded in 2005 under the direction of Dr. Drew Davidson, the Director of Carnegie Mellon University's Entertainment Technology Center (ETC), as an open access, digital-first publishing house.

What does all that mean?

The ETC Press publishes three types of work:peer-reviewed work (research-based books, textbooks, academic journals, conference proceedings), general audience work (trade nonfiction, singles, Well Played singles), and research and white papers

The common tie for all of these is a focus on issues related to entertainment technologies as they are applied across a variety of fields.

Our authors come from a range of backgrounds. Some are traditional academics. Some are practitioners. And some work in between. What ties them all together is their ability to write about the impact of emerging technologies and its significance in society.

To distinguish our books, the ETC Press has five imprints:

- **ETC Press:** our traditional academic and peer-reviewed publications;

- **ETC Press: Single:** our short "why it matters" books that are roughly 8,000-25,000 words;

- **ETC Press: Signature:** our special projects, trade books, and other curated works that exemplify the best work being done;

- **ETC Press: Report:** our white papers and reports produced by practitioners or academic researchers working in conjunction with partners; and

- **ETC Press: Student:** our work with undergraduate and graduate students

In keeping with that mission, the ETC Press uses emerging technologies to design all of our books and Lulu, an on-demand publisher, to distribute our e-books and print books through all the major retail chains, such as Amazon, Barnes & Noble, Kobo, and Apple, and we work with The Game Crafter to produce tabletop games.

We don't carry an inventory ourselves. Instead, each print book is created when somebody buys a copy.

Since the ETC Press is an open-access publisher, every book, journal, and proceeding is available as a free download. We're most interested in the sharing and spreading of ideas. We also have an agreement with the Association for Computing Machinery (ACM) to list ETC Press publications in the ACM Digital Library.

Authors retain ownership of their intellectual property. We release all of our books, journals, and proceedings under one of two Creative Commons licenses:

- **Attribution-NoDerivativeWorks-NonCommercial:** This license allows for published works to remain intact, but versions can be created; or

- **Attribution-NonCommercial-ShareAlike:** This license allows for authors to retain editorial control of their creations while also encouraging readers to collaboratively rewrite content.

This is definitely an experiment in the notion of publishing, and we invite people to participate. We are exploring what it means to "publish" across multiple media and multiple versions. We believe this is the future of publication, bridging virtual and physical media with fluid versions of publications as well as enabling the creative blurring of what constitutes reading and writing.

www.ingramcontent.com/pod-product-compliance
Lightning Source LLC
Chambersburg PA
CBHW071229220526
45468CB00002B/777